D1096323

THE FIRST WORLD WAR
A PHOTOGRAPHIC HISTORY

EDITED
WITH CAPTIONS
AND AN INTRODUCTION
BY

LAURENCE STALLINGS

1933
NEW YORK

SIMON AND SCHUSTER

THE FIRST WORLD WAR, A PHOTOGRAPHIC HISTORY

FIRST PRINTING, August, 1933

MANUFACTURED IN U. S. A.

THIS ENTIRE BOOK HAS BEEN PRINTED IN OFFSET LITHOGRAPHY BY MORTIMER AND WALLING, NEW YORK, FROM DEEP-ETCHED OFFSET PLATES BY SWART-REICHEL INC., NEW YORK
BINDING BY H. WOLFF ESTATE, NEW YORK

Dedicated to

THE CAMERA EYE

Additional explanatory captions for a number of the photographs in THE FIRST WORLD WAR will be found in the back of this book

PUBLISHERS' FOREWORD

ALMOST three years of research work, both in Europe and America, have gone into the making of this photographic chronicle of the World War.

Many of the pictures are here published for the first time. Many come from the pictorial sections, historical staffs, and war colleges of the principal powers—naturally from both sides. Some come from Signal Corps photographers of the American Expeditionary Forces; some from similar European sources; some from individual participants and eye-witnesses, professional as well as amateur; still others from war correspondents, newspaper photographers, commercial news services, books, magazines, and newspapers here and abroad.

Mr. Otto Kurth, formerly art editor of the *New York Times Mid-Week Pictorial*, cartographer and picture editor of several histories of the World War, together with the publishers themselves and a staff of assistants, supervised the assembly of these thousands of pictures.

After painstaking appraisal and selection, the best of these photographs—and only those of unimpeachable authenticity—were finally chosen, and, under the direction of both editors and publishers, arranged in chronological, integrated order.

As general editor, Mr. Laurence Stallings advised the technical editor and the publishers on the basic pattern of the book, consulted with them on the main points of emphasis, wrote the captions for the pictures, checked the layouts and wrote the introduction.

The captions prepared by Mr. Stallings are designed not only to indicate the march of time but to suggest the moods and backgrounds of the War in all its phases. Wherever possible, the editors have supplied, in the back of the book, further factual data on the pictures in the form of supplementary captions for reference purposes. Readers desiring to have this specific information on particular photographs will find them numerically indexed in the back of the book under the corresponding page numbers.

In the back of the book will also be found a summary of reprint credit acknowledgments and copyright designations. So far as possible the editors and publishers tried to obtain photographs from primary sources, but in many cases this was of course impossible. The research work was so extensive that exact citation and acknowledgment represented many difficulties, but the most conscientious effort has been made to give full credit to the original source, where known.

To list, even in the briefest possible manner, the names of all the persons who have helped with citations, suggestions, and actual pictures would require more space than is here available. But the publishers wish to record their profound gratitude to the photographers, known and unknown, who took the pictures here presented, and to both the general editor, Mr. Laurence Stallings, and the technical editor, Mr. Otto Kurth, for their indefatigable and inspired labors. They are also deeply grateful to all the co-operating publishers, editors, news services, and photographic bureaus, both here and abroad, as listed in the back of the book. No record of thanks and acknowledgment would be complete without a special salute to Captain B. H. Liddell Hart, author of "The Real War"; Mr. Douglas Jerrold, author of "The War on Land"; Captain F. W. Hoorn, Signal Corps, Army Pictorial Service, Washington, D. C.; Mr. F. A. Barber, Historical Foundations, New York City; Major C. C. Benson, Secretary, Historical Section, Army War College, Washington, D. C.; Colonel Kendall Banning, formerly Chief of the Army Pictorial Service, General Staff, Washington, D. C.; Mr. Reed Chambers; Mrs. Cockburn-Lange; Captain Dudley Knox, U. S. Navy; Captain J. H. Craige, U. S. Marine Corps; the Secretary of the Imperial War Museum of Great Britain, and the Under-Secretary of State, British War Office; Professor James T. Shotwell, Columbia University; Rear Admiral T. J. Cowie, U. S. N.; Major Clarence Lovejoy, U. S. A.; Mr. Meredith Wood; Mr. Chester Eskey; Herr Andor Braun, of Vienna and New York; Mr. Norman Collins, of London; Mr. Harry Hoffman; Miss Bertha Hunt; Mr. and Mrs. Leon Shimkin; Miss Helen Jepson; the editors of Frankfurter Societäts Druckerei, Frankfurt am Main; Herr Oscar Tellgmann; Hofphotograph Carl Eberth; Signor Guido Almagia.

IF IT is true that one picture is worth a thousand words, the publishers hope that this photographic chronicle, arranged as it is in the most dramatic possible sequence (chronological) and freed from all national prejudices and temporary taboos of censorship, may supplement the other forms of war history "as a record, as visual excitement, as a bald-faced reckoning of the costs." This work is offered, not as history, but as a graphic aid to history. In a mere five hundred pictures, it is obviously impossible to give even an infinitesimal fraction of a detailed account of the War. But the camera can disclose, within these limitations of space, the high points, the pivotal events, the crucial situations.

We are now sufficiently removed from the clash of arms to attain something like a total perspective. We know now that the World War began long before 1914, and continued long after 1918. We know now that it was not fought by men of war alone.

No national partisanship, no special pleading, no desire either to glorify or to attack, guided the compilers of this book. History, says Santayana, is merely memory aided and directed. In that spirit, this volume is added to the already stupendous literature of the World War.

There have been other photographic records of the War, but they have been either voluminous or inaccessible portfolios, loosely-assembled albums, or technical departmentalized books, devoted to one country, one phase, one battle-front, or one arm of the service. Here we attempt to give a kaleidoscopic, panoramic impression of totality, to show glimpses of the larger causes and effects, vistas of that

"*. . . darkling plain*
Swept with confused alarms of struggle and flight,
Where ignorant armies clash by night. . . ."

M. LINCOLN SCHUSTER.

INTRODUCTION

By Laurence Stallings

In this anthology of pictures of the first world war there was no effort to satisfy any special interest or taste. A militarist will be disappointed in them, for there are not enough pictures of guns and tactical groups. A pacifist will not find enough horror, nor enough of cadavers. And a student of war can hardly follow, from these pictorial representations, the methods of infantry combat slowly evolving from close-packed slaughter of the trenches to the loosely-held butcheries later on. Any such special book can be made when the various war colleges publish their *pictures; though one doubts that any now living generation will be booned such a sight.*

Some of the photographs in this collection are as good as film can make them, while others are obviously lacking in composition and detail. But who might set a stop or calculate an exposure in, for example, a wheatfield dripping with blood? The unbelievable thing is—that some men did, and lived to develop the negative and print the picture. These photographers are mainly nameless; but one must conjecture about them: a wit photographed those Russians running pell-mell, and a humanist caught those sad exiles in the cart, and only a cat among camera men could have looked so long at a king who sits, a draggled eagle, morosely watching his armies scatter before Mackensen's vans. But who caught the sad file of prisoners bearing that comrade with the Homeric thrust over the left nipple? (Homer made a cliché of that particular wound.) And the non-commissioned officer in the left foreground is smiling? At whom?

Many of these pictures hold a secret, as securely as the dead hold theirs. Others are official, and many others are thoughtless. They are all, I believe, genuine.

The editor is conscious of his short-comings in the matter of captions. Many should be more expert, more military. A military expert, to paraphrase, is one who carefully avoids all the small errors as he sweeps on to the grand fallacy. This book, at least, avoids that fallacy. There is no conclusion to it. Man made this world in four years, and saw that it was good, if we are to believe Versailles. Well, here it is in the making, just as man made it, caught by many a camera eye. The pictures are placed more or less chronologically, but for the most part in a senseless fashion. Who, looking on them, can give the riddle of them? Perhaps they are not embracing enough: that matter of Africa's absence perplexes; for more Negroes were killed there in 1914-18 than were slaughtered in the previous hundred years of tribal warfare. There should be more pictures of Africa? In the next war, experts assure us, there will be. Africa's injured pride must take the promise as a sop.

The main theatre of the camera is Europe. The pictures, if they prove anything, offer testimony that the first world war was mainly a duel between the German armies and those of France and Russia. This is not to say that the British by 1917 had not developed a first rate military power and were not killing and being killed by millions; nor that Italy was left out of the book; nor America. But the bulk of the photographs are from the main event—the war on land, and the land, Europe. The publishers with invincible energy have endeavored to collect pictures from every angle of that conflict; for just as war is no longer a matter of soldiers, the pictures from them have equally enlarged the view. There have been several collections of war pictures, and these mostly compiled with a taste for horror. Every nice distinction has been observed in this matter here; and only an occasional photograph recalls that, whatever else happened in the general insanity of the time, men were rotting away like hay in the fields of the world.

At first the editorial board hoped to be more exact in the matter of definition and legend. Surely some of these pictures had a direct bearing on the world of Ludendorff, Haig, Foch—to name three giants of that day on earth. But what bearing these had on the events to follow is still a moot question. And if this picture book survives, doubtless it will get in time another preface, and one which will make sense out of chaos. In the meantime, here is the camera record of chaos, with the reader annoyed by only the briefest captions.

THE

FIRST WORLD WAR

A PHOTOGRAPHIC HISTORY

"THE BALANCE OF POWER" — 1815

PEACE CONFERENCE AT THE HAGUE — 1883

"BLOOD AND IRON" — 1870

"SPHERES OF INFLUENCE" — 1906

IMPERIAL GERMANY TURNS EASTWARD . . .

KRUPP WORKS SPEED UP . . .

BRITAIN BUILDS MORE SHIPS . . .

FRANCE CLAMORS FOR GUNS . . .

"All the News That's Fit to Print."

The New York Times.

THE WEATHER
Local showers today; Tuesday, fair; fresh, shifting winds, becoming northwest.

VOL. LXIII...NO. 20,610. NEW YORK, MONDAY, JUNE 29, 1914.—EIGHTEEN PAGES. ONE CENT

HEIR TO AUSTRIA'S THRONE IS SLAIN WITH HIS WIFE BY A BOSNIAN YOUTH TO AVENGE SEIZURE OF HIS COUNTRY

Francis Ferdinand Shot During State Visit to Sarajevo.

TWO ATTACKS IN A DAY

Archduke Saves His Life First Time by Knocking Aside a Bomb Hurled at Auto.

SLAIN IN SECOND ATTEMPT

Lad Dashes at Car as the Royal Couple Return from Town Hall and Kills Both of Them.

LAID TO A SERVIAN PLOT

Heir Warned Not to Go to Bosnia, Where Populace Met Him with Servian Flags.

AGED EMPER... ...RICKEN

Archduke Francis Ferdinand and his Consort the Duchess of Hohenberg Slain by Assassin's Bullets.

...could only certify they were both dead.

The authors of both attacks upon the Archduke are born Bosnians. Gabrinovics is a compositor, and worked for a few weeks in the Government ... at Belgrade. He re-...

...by splinters from the bomb. Several persons on the pavement were very seriously hurt by the explosion of the bomb, which was thrown by a young man named Tabrinovitch, (Gabrinovics,) who is a typist from Trebenie in Herzegovina, and is of ... tionality...

It is feared that it will lead to serious complications with that unruly kingdom, and may have far-reaching results. The future of the ... subject of ...

CALIFORNIA GOES ON ROCKS IN FOG

...ry Island, Off Northwest Irish Coast, Scene of Mishap to Anchor Liner.

NO IMMEDIATE DANGER

...ws Badly Stove In and Ship Taking Water Through Two Holes in Hold.

...SSENGERS STILL ABOARD

STAYS IN AIR 21 HOURS.

Berlin Aviator's Feat Held to be a World's Record.

BERLIN, June 28.—Herr Landmann, an aviator, today concluded a non-stop flight of 21 hours 48 minutes.

It is asserted that this flight constitutes a world record.

Twenty-one hours would be almost enough to carry the seaplane America either to the coast of Ireland, or to the Azores. Plans for the forthcoming trans-Atlantic flight are based on the America's reaching the Azores in twenty hours.

DEWEY IN CANAL PARADE.

Will Be Invited to Make Trip Aboard His Old Flagship Olympia.

Special to The New York Times.

WASHINGTON, June 28.—Admiral George Dewey may take his old flagship, the Olympia, through the Panama Canal next March in the naval parade. Rear Admiral Clark, retired, has been ordered to take command of his old ship, the Oregon, for the occasion, and Secretary...

FEDERALS DESERT AGUASCALIENTES

Town South of Zacatecas Evacuated by Huerta's Forces, but Villa Turns Back.

IS CAMPAIGN ABANDONED?

Border Hears His Ammunition Is Exhausted — Row with Carranza Will Not Down.

ENVOYS WAIT ON CARRANZA

Propose Pan-American Memorial to Columbus

A splendid tomb topped by a great light is proposed to be erected in Santo Domingo, in the Caribbean Sea, by subscriptions from peoples of all lands. See NEXT SUNDAY'S TIMES.

OUR GUNS FIRE ON SANTO DOMINGO

Few Shots from the Machias Stop Bombardment of Puerto Plata by President Bordas.

Neue

Freie Presse.

Morgenblatt.

Nr. 17903. Wien, Montag, den 29. Juni 1914.

† Erzherzog Franz Ferdinand.

Der Thronfolger und seine Gemahlin ermordet.

PRINCIP LIGHTS THE FUSE

TUNIC OF THE MURDERED ARCHDUKE

An das Deutsche Volk.

Seit der Reichsgründung ist es durch 43 Jahre Mein und Meiner Vorfahren heißes Bemühen gewesen, der Welt den Frieden zu erhalten und im Frieden unsere kraftvolle Entwickelung zu fördern. Aber die Gegner neiden uns den Erfolg unserer Arbeit.

Alle offenkundige und heimliche Feindschaft von Ost und West, von jenseits der See haben wir bisher ertragen im Bewußtsein unserer Verantwortung und Kraft. Nun aber will man uns demütigen. Man verlangt, daß wir mit verschränkten Armen zusehen, wie unsere Feinde sich zu tückischem Überfall rüsten, man will nicht dulden, daß wir in entschlossener Treue zu unserem Bundesgenossen stehen, der um sein Ansehen als Großmacht kämpft und mit dessen Erniedrigung auch unsere Macht und Ehre verloren ist.

So muß denn das Schwert entscheiden. Mitten im Frieden überfällt uns der Feind. Darum auf! zu den Waffen! Jedes Schwanken, jedes Zögern wäre Verrat am Vaterlande.

Um Sein oder Nichtsein unseres Reiches handelt es sich, das unsere Väter ne sich gründeten. Um Sein oder Nichtsein deutscher Macht und deutschen Wesens.

Wir werden uns wehren bis zum letzten Hauch von Mann und Roß. Und w werden diesen Kampf bestehen auch gegen eine Welt von Feinden. Noch nie wa Deutschland überwunden, wenn es einig war.

Vorwärts mit Gott, der mit uns sein wird, wie er mit den Vätern wa

Berlin, den 6. August 1914.

Wilhelm.

GREAT BRITAIN DECLARES WAR ON GERMANY.

SUMMARY REJECTION OF BRITISH ULTIMATUM.

ALL EYES ON THE NORTH

INVASION OF

HOME FLEETS.

SUPREME COMMAND.

SIR JOHN JELLICOE, K.C.B.

THE KING'S MESSAGE TO THE FLEET.

TWO MORE BRITISH DREADNOUGHTS.

ACQUISITION FROM TURKEY.

4.0 a.m. EDITION.

New York Tribune

NEW YORK, WEDNESDAY, JULY 29, 1914.

PRICE ONE CENT

AUSTRIA DECLARES WAR, RUSHES VAST ARMY INTO SERVIA; RUSSIA MASSES 80,000 MEN ON BORDER

Grey's Plan for London Peace Conference Is Abandoned, While War Spirit Fills Continental Capitals.

GERMANY READY ON SEA AND LAND

AUSTRO-SERVIAN FRONTIER.

WAR SHOCKS STOCK MARKET; GOLD GOES OUT

CAILLAUX FREED WITH CRY OF "MURDERESS"

Morgen-Ausgabe

Berliner Tageblatt

und Handels-Zeitung

Sonnabend 1. August 1914

Ultimatum an Rußland – Anfrage an Frankreich.

Deutschland während seiner Vermittlungsaktion von Russland bedroht. – Ansprache des Kaisers an das Volk. – Trauung des Prinzen Oskar. – Verlobung des Prinzen Adalbert.

The World.

VOL. LV. NO. 19,341.

"Circulation Books Open to All."

NEW YORK, TUESDAY, AUGUST 4, 1914.

Two Great Armies Meet!

BRITAIN ON VERGE OF WAR WITH GERMANY; GERMANS INVADE HOLLAND; FIGHT AT SEA; GOLD OUTFLOW STOPS; BILLION MORE MONEY

CLEARING HOUSE STOPS RAID

GERMANY INVADES HOLLAND; NATION PREPARES DEFENSE

Sir Edward Grey Tells House of Commons German Navy Will Not Be Allowed to Attack France—Threat of Kaiser to Invade Belgium Causes

60me Année – 3me Série – N° 216

Gaston CALMETTE

LE FIGARO

Le Numéro quotidien : DIX CENTIMES en France et en Belgique – Étranger : VINGT CENTIMES

Les Neutralités violées

La guerre déclarée

L'Allemagne

DÉCLARATION DE SIR EDWARD GREY

"HOW STILL THIS QUIET CORN-FIELD IS TO-NIGHT"

DEUTSCHLAND ÜBER ALLES!

RULE BRITANNIA!

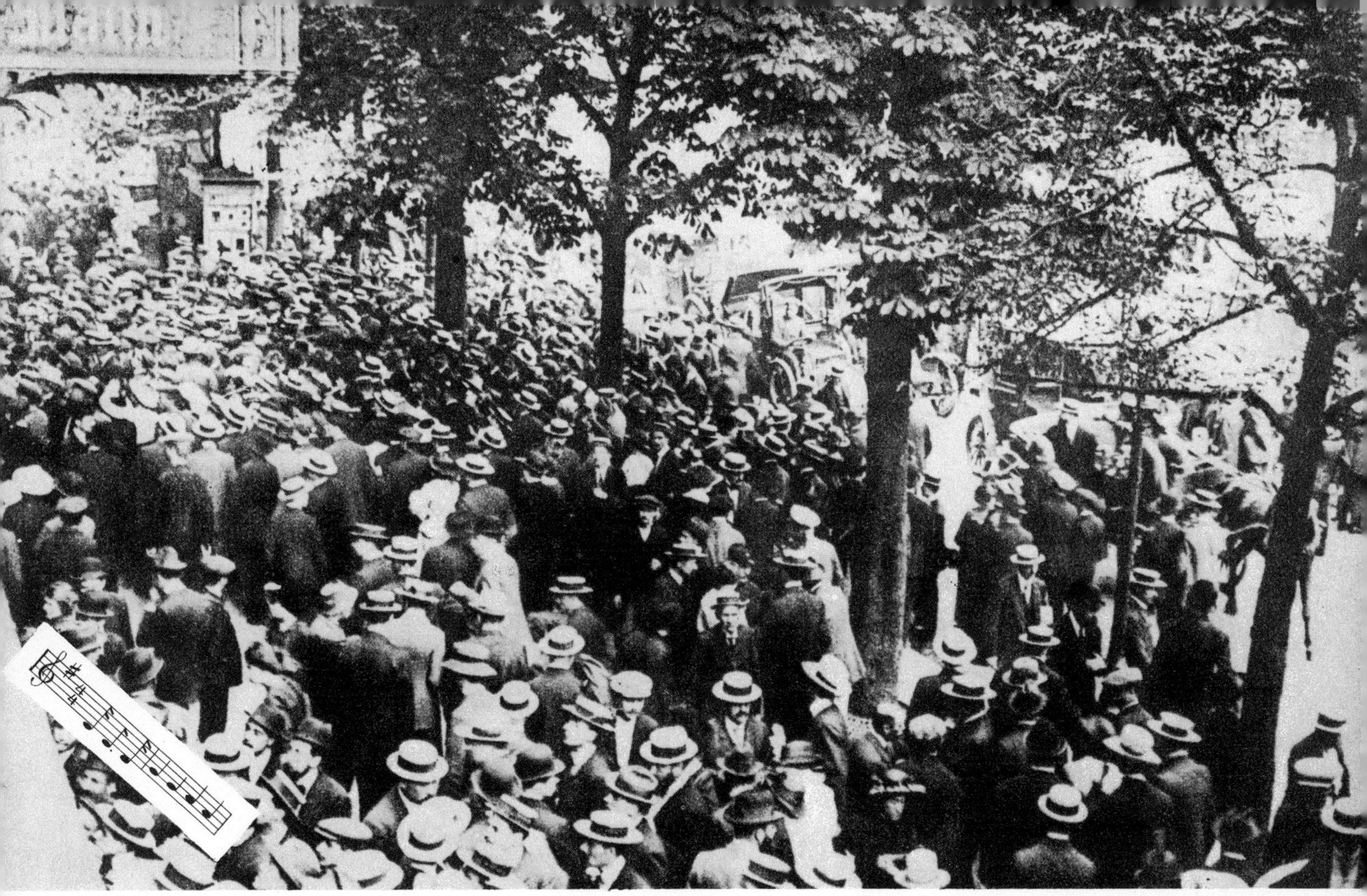

VIVE LA FRANCE!

ZDRAVO, SRBI!

ALL ABOARD FOR PARIS

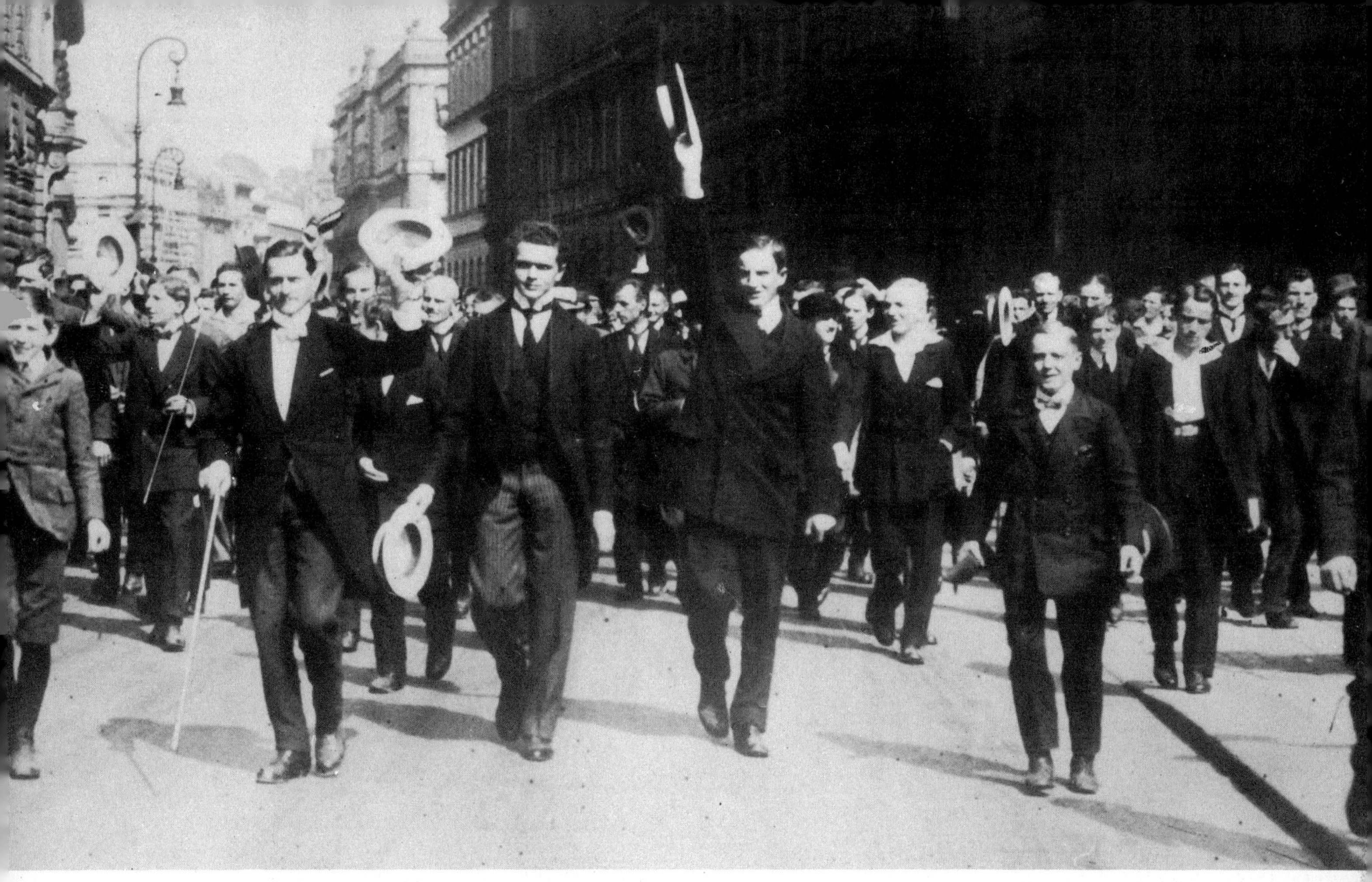

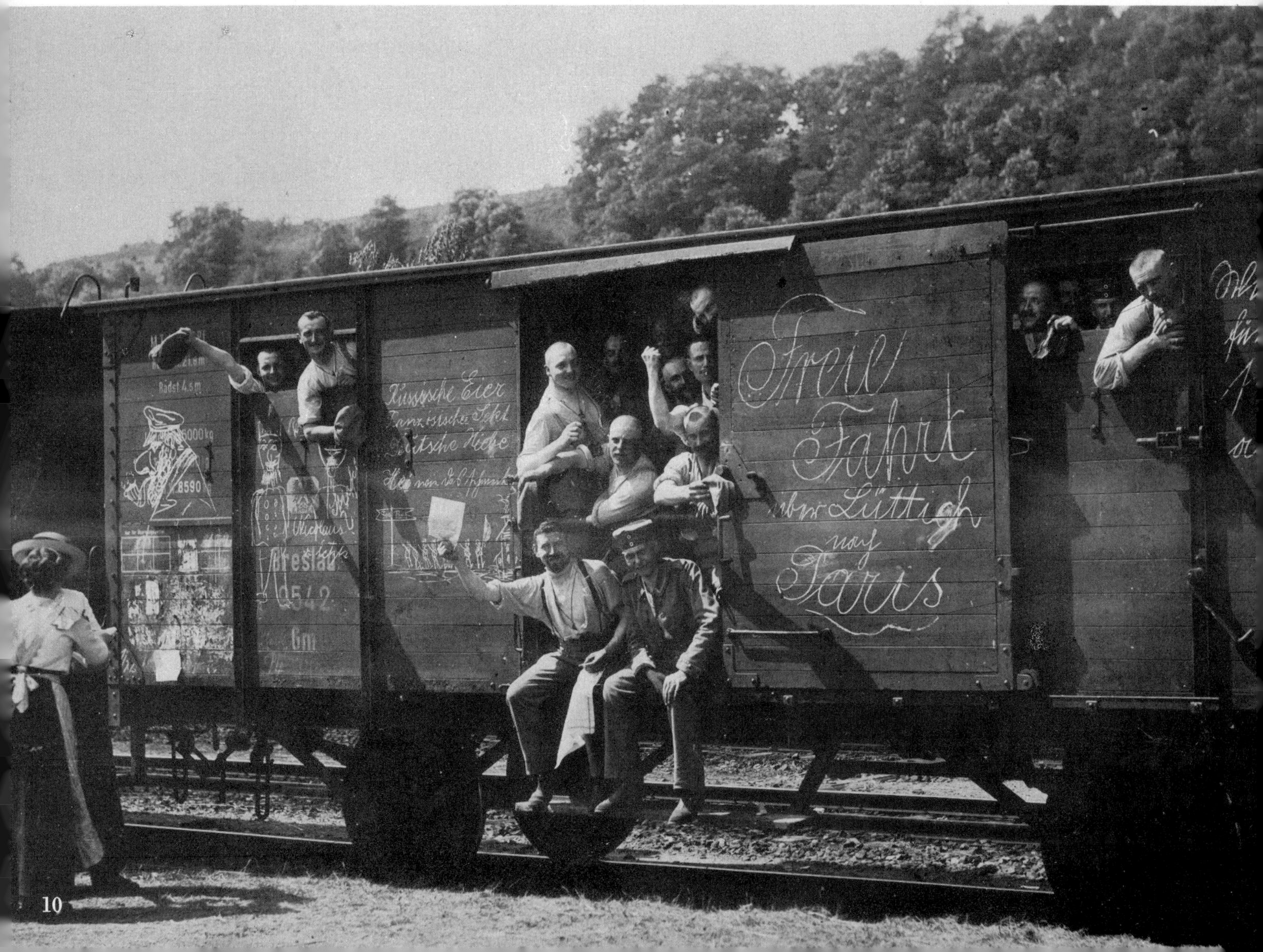
Freie
Fahrt
über Lüttich
nach
Paris

AU REVOIR!

AUF WIEDERSEHEN!

GOOD-BYE!

RESERVISTS: NEW YORK TO BERLIN

GOVERNORS CLOSE STOCK EXCHANGE

Other Exchanges Also Shut to Check Europe's Dumping of Securities Here.

STOP GOLD'S OUTFLOW NEXT

Washington to Facilitate Issue of $500,000,000 Additional Bank Circulation.

TOURISTS: BERLIN TO NEW YORK

TRAVELLERS: DOVER TO HAMBURG

". . . WHEN SHALL I SEE THE THIN SAD SLATES THAT COVER UP MY HOME?"

BRUSSELS: A RECEPTION COMMITTEE . . .

. . . THE GUESTS ARRIVE

SIEGE GUN

HOTEL MONICO
HOTEL MONICO
CIGARES
VAN CUTSEM MONICO
MONICO

BRUSSELS FALLS, AUGUST 20, 1914

"AND THE BRAVEST OF THESE ARE THE BELGIANS"

GOOSE STEP IN ANTWERP

"RANGE!"

REFUGEES: BELGIUM TO ENGLAND

"TAKE ARMS AGAINST A SEA OF TROUBLES . . ."

PRISONERS OF WAR

NO TRESPASSING!

OSTEND: BRITISH MARINES HAVE LANDED

ETON: TEACHING THE YOUNG IDEA TO SHOOT

TROOPING OF THE COLORS

SERVE
YOUR COUNTRY
OR
WEAR THIS

"O WHAT CAN AIL THEE, KNIGHT-AT-ARMS?"

MINOR TACTICS IN A LONDON STREET

"A MIGHTY FORTRESS IS OUR GOD"

FORWARDING ADDRESS

"E'EN NOW THE DEVASTATION IS BEGUN,
AND HALF THE BUSINESS OF DESTRUCTION DONE . . ."

"ALL QUIET ON THE EASTERN FRONT"

RAPE OF BELGIUM

FRENCH VIEW

NEUTRAL AMERICA

"THE ALLIES HAVE GAINED THEIR FIRST IMPORTANT VICTORY IN THE EAST: THE RUSSIANS HAVE ENTERED LEMBERG"

"THE GRAND DUKE NICHOLAS HAS LOST, IN PRISONERS ALONE, 750,000 MEN"

CASUALTY LIST

"NAME? RANK? REGIMENT? NUMBER?"

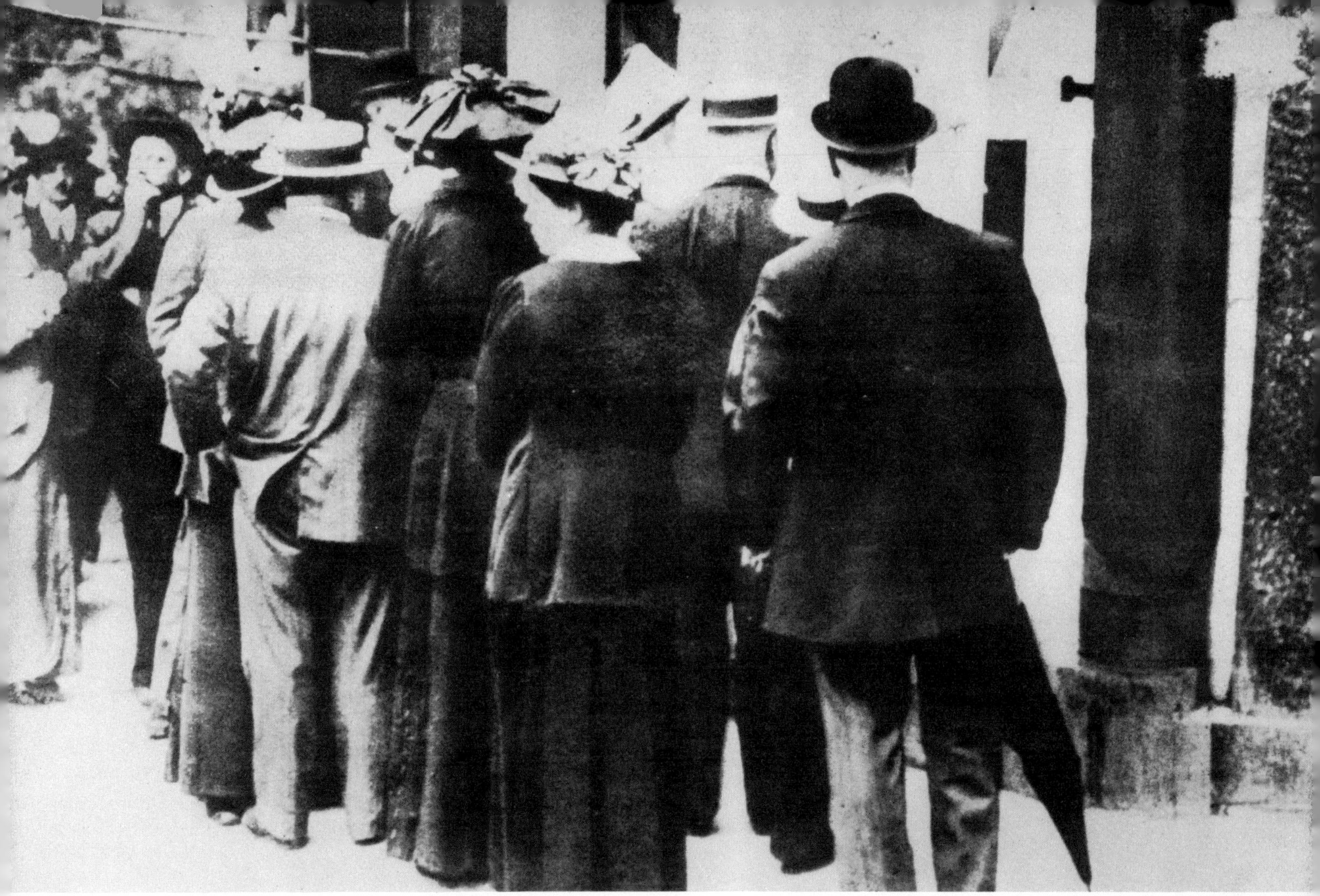

CASUALTY LIST

"NAME? RANK? REGIMENT? NUMBER?"

Weather Forecast: FAIR, COOLER.

Rushing to the Goal!
3,137 World Ads. Yesterday
1,840 MORE THAN THE HERALD
Trump, Trump, Trump, World Ads. Are Marching

The World.

"Circulation Books Open to All."

"Circulation Books Open to All."

WEATHER FORECAST

OUTING KIT

IN NEXT SUNDAY'S WORLD

VOL. LV. NO. 19,372. NEW YORK, FRIDAY, SEPTEMBER 4, 1914. PRICE

PARIS HASTENS TO THROW UP NEW DEFENSES; GERMANS CUT OFF FLIGHT TO NORTH COAST; 4,758 BRITISH MISSING IN NEW LOSS REPORT.

NEW POPE IS BENEDICT XV. | RUSSIANS HOLDING | FLEET OF AIRSHIPS | BRITISH GOT ... FROM | Valley of the S... Abandoned by the Allies

THEY HAD TO SEE PARIS

"ICH HATTE EINST EIN SCHÖNES VATERLAND; ES WAR EIN TRAUM . . ."

"All the News That's Fit to Print."

The New York Times.

THE WEATHER
Fair, cooler today; threatening tomorrow; brisk northwest winds.

VOL. LXIII. NO. 20,681. NEW YORK, TUESDAY, SEPTEMBER 8, 1914.—EIGHTEEN PAGES. ONE CENT In Greater New York, Jersey City and Newark. Elsewhere TWO CENTS.

GERMANS PUSHED BACK IN 160-MILE BATTLE; IMPERIAL GUARD IS REPORTED CUT TO PIECES; NEW ALLIED ARMY IS PROBABLY IN ACTION

AUSTRIAN ARMY IN DEADLY TRAP

Officially Reported by Petrograd to be Retreating with Great Losses.

CAMPAIGN MAY COLLAPSE

Przemysl, the Last Remaining Stronghold in Galicia, Being Invested by Invaders.

Summary of War News

PATHFINDER LOST 246 OF HER MEN

Roll of Cruiser Sunk by Mine Shows 242 Missing, Admiralty Reports.

VESSEL BLOWN TO ATOMS

And Sank in Four Minutes While Her Wireless Was Calling to Fleet for Aid.

GERMANS' MARCH ON PARIS

Philip Gibbs the Novelist Tells How It Was Met and Deflected

ALLIES TAKE OFFENSIVE

Advance, Driving Back the Germans [illegible] Northeast

Germany Again Reported Ready for Peace; Mr. Straus Confers with Mr. Bryan and Diplomats

CRITICAL MOMENT IN PARIS

"ICH HATT' EINEN KAMERADEN"

MACHINE GUN, ATTENDED

DIRECT HIT

SANDBAGS

THE MARNE: EARLY AUTUMN

"LET EVERY MAN CARRY TWO EXTRA BANDOLIERS"

LA BELLE FRANCE

"SUFFER LITTLE CHILDREN . . ."

SEA MONSTER

The New York Times.

"All the News That's Fit to Print."

THE WEATHER
Rain Thursday; fair, cold wave by night Friday.

VOL. LXVI. NO. 21,558. NEW YORK, THURSDAY, FEBRUARY 1, 1917.—TWENTY-TWO PAGES. ONE CENT

GERMANY BEGINS RUTHLESS SEA WARFARE; DRAWS 'BARRED ZONES' AROUND THE ALLIES; CRISIS CONFRONTS THE UNITED STATES

THIS PORT CLOSED

Text of Germany's Note to the United States

A SHIP A WEEK FOR US

RETREAT: CLOSE-UP OF A BALKAN KING

DESERTED VILLAGE

SIESTA

THESE GERMANS REACHED ENGLAND

THESE FRENCHMEN REACHED GERMANY

DIVINE GUIDANCE

FOOD FOR THE GUNS

CRUCIFIX

Another Call
"MORE MEN AND STILL MORE UNTIL THE ENEMY IS CRUSHED"
LORD KITCHENER.

MEN OF LONDON
NOW IS THE TIME
Nearest Recruiting Office:
Holborn Hall.
"The British Empire is fighting for its existence."
-Lord Kitchener.
"I shall want more men and still more until the enemy is crushed."
Lord Kitchener.
Come forward now and be trained to do your share.
Every fit man owes this duty to himself and to his country.

ENLIST TO-I

THERE'S ROOM FOR YOU
ENLIST TO-DAY
ENGLAND EXPECTS
EVERY MAN TO DO HIS DUTY

THE KEY TO THE
MUNITIONS
MEN AND MONEY
ARE YOU HELPING TO TURN IT?
SITUATION

"THAT OLD, UNDYING SIN WE SHARED IN ROUEN MARKET PLACE"

SHAMBLES AT PRZEMYSL

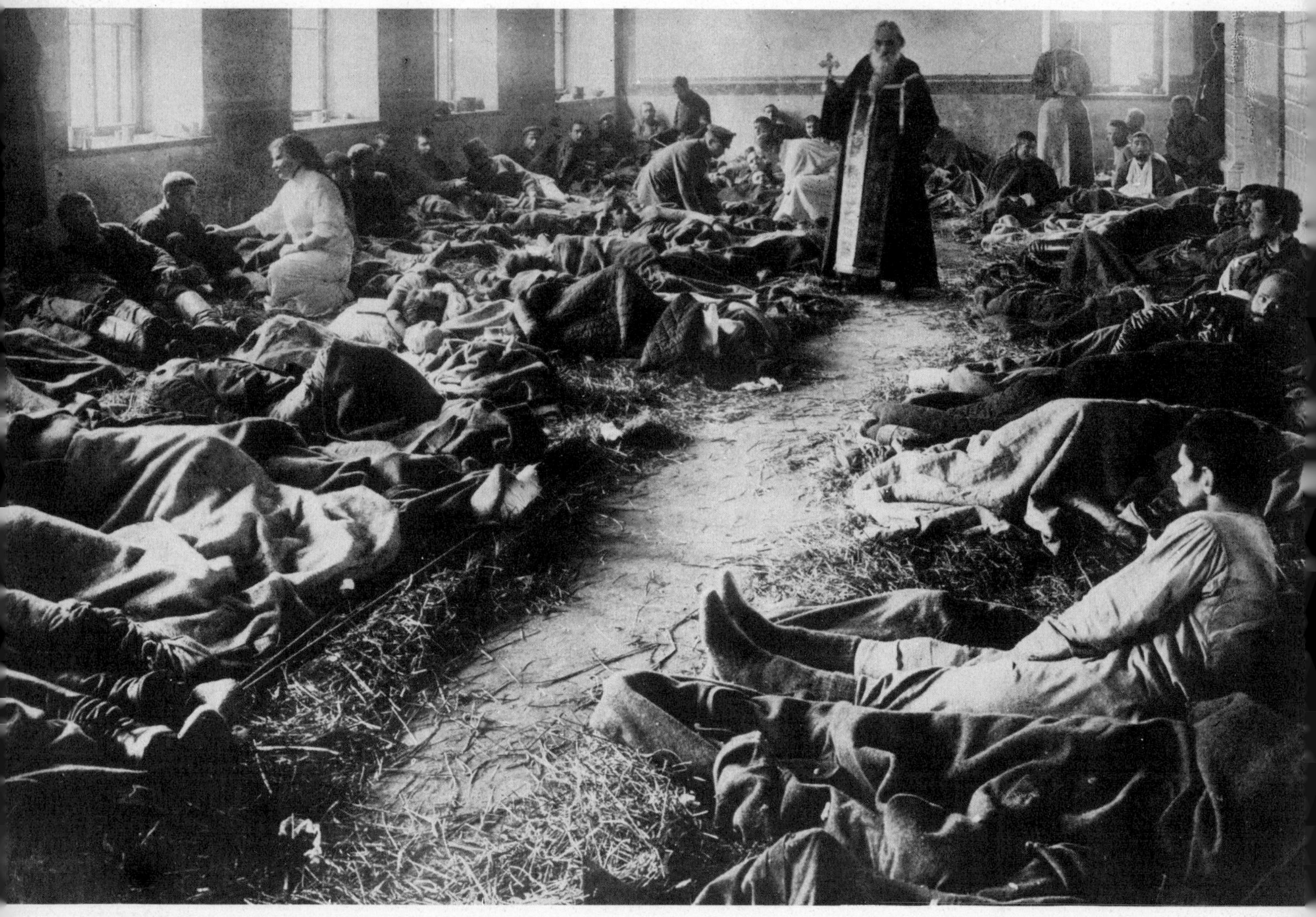

RUSSIANS IN CHURCH

". . . KEEP THE HOME FIRES BURNING . . ."

BYSTANDERS IN EAST PRUSSIA

"IT MAY BE HE SHALL FIND ME STILL"

CASUALTY LISTS: BERLIN

POLISH CROSS

BRITANNIA RULES THE WAVES

END OF A RAIDER

"ABANDON SHIP!"

GERMAN SHOP IN LONDON

64

"All the News That's Fit to Print."

The New York Times.

EXTRA
5:30 A. M.

VOL. LXIV...NO. 20,923. NEW YORK, SATURDAY, MAY 8, 1915.—TWENTY-FOUR PAGES. ONE CENT In Greater New York, Jersey City and Newark. | Elsewhere TWO CENTS.

LUSITANIA SUNK BY A SUBMARINE, PROBABLY 1,260 DEAD; TWICE TORPEDOED OFF IRISH COAST; SINKS IN 15 MINUTES; CAPT. TURNER SAVED, FROHMAN AND VANDERBILT MISSING; WASHINGTON BELIEVES THAT A GRAVE CRISIS IS AT HAND

SHOCKS THE PRESIDENT

Washington Deeply Stirred by the Loss of American Lives.

BULLETINS AT WHITE HOUSE

Wilson Reads Them Closely, but Is Silent on the Nation's Course.

HINTS OF CONGRESS CALL

Loss of Lusitania Recalls Firm Tone of Our First Warn-

The Lost Cunard Steamship Lusitania

SOME DEAD TAKEN ASHORE

Several Hundred Survivors at Queenstown and Kinsale.

STEWARD TELLS OF DISASTER

...pedo Crashes Into the

...ged for News; ...nia Long in Doubt

...Known Passengers on ...ong Unconfirmed ...eek Details.

List of Saved Includes Capt. Turner; Vanderbilt and Frohman Reported Lost

LONDON, Saturday, May 8, 5:30 A. M.—The Press Bureau has received from the British Admiralty at Queenstown a report that all the torpedo boats and tugs and armed trawlers, except the Heron, which went out from Queenstown to the relief of the Lusitania have returned.

These vessels have landed 595 survivors and forty dead. Fifty-two more survivors are reported aboard a steamer, while eleven others and five bodies have been landed at Kinsale, making the total number of survivors 658, besides forty-five dead. The numbers will be verified later, and it is considered possible Kinsale fishing boats may have rescued a few more.

Among the survivors is the Captain of the Lusitania, William T. Turner. Some of the survivors at Queenstown say that Alfred Gwynne ...

Saw the Submarine 100 Y... and Watched Torpedo as...

Ernest Cowper, a Toronto Newspa... Attack, Seen from Ship's Rai... Used in Torpedoes, Say Othe...

Queenstown, Saturday, May 8, 3:18 A. M.

A sharp lookout for submarines was kept aboard the Lusitania as she approached

ADVERTISEMENT.

NOTICE!

TRAVELLERS intending to embark on the Atlantic voyage are reminded that a state of war exists between Germany and her allies and Great Britain and her allies; that the zone of war includes the waters adjacent to the British Isles; that, in accordance with formal notice given by the Imperial German Government, vessels flying the flag of Great Britain, or of any of her allies, are liable to destruction in those waters and that travellers sailing in the war zone on ships of Great Britain or her allies do so at their own risk.

IMPERIAL GERMAN EMBASSY
WASHINGTON, D. C., APRIL 22, 1915.

A VILLAGE HEEDS THE RUMBLE OF A DISTANT DRUM

MOUNTAINS IN ITALY

MACHINE GUN: AUSTRIAN MAKE

RAIDING PARTY

Stadt München

Brotkarte A

Nicht übertragbar! | Rückseite beachten! | Unveräußerlich!

Die Karte berechtigt zum Einkauf

von 14 Pfund Brot
oder 10 Pfund Brot und 3 Pfund Mehl
ferner von ½ Pfund Reis

in der Zeit
vom 29. November bis 26. Dezember 1915
(4 Wochen).

Für verloren gegangene oder zu früh verbrauchte Karten werden neue Karten **nicht** abgegeben.

BERLIN: SOUP AT THE ORPHANAGE

BON de 40 centimes

pour un pain D'UN KILO, poids net

ou pour un seau de charbon de 12 kilos
ou pour 4 kilos de pommes de terre
ou pour 1/4 de kilog. de margarine.

à prendre dans les dépôts communaux et pas ailleurs.

Ce bon est aussi valable pour l'achat, n'importe où, d'autres articles de première nécessité.

Il ... nal de
(bure... ture du

Mehlkarte
der Stadt München

Nicht übertragbar! | **Rückseite beachten!** | Unveräusserlich!

Die Karte berechtigt zum Einkauf von **2 Pfund Mehl** in der Zeit vom 14. Juni bis 8. August 1915 (8 Wochen). Für verloren gegangene oder zu früh verbrauchte Karten werden neue Karten **nicht** abgegeben.

Eigenhändige Unterschrift des verfügungsberechtigten Inhabers der Karte (Haushaltungsvorstand, Familienhaupt u. s. w.)

Gegen nicht unterzeichnete Karten darf kein Mehl verkauft werden.

GERMANY'S SUPPLY OF FOOD LIMITLESS

Count von Bernstorff Says Country Is Absolutely Self-Sustaining.

CONSULTS ABOUT WIRELESS

Ambassador Says of Zeppelin Bomb Attack on Antwerp That Hospital Was Inside a Fortress.

VILLE DE SPA

31-7-15

0,20

payables par la caisse communale aussitôt le rétablissement de la situation normale

K 30174

Le Receveur, Le Secrétaire, Le Bourgmestre,

SPA. IMP. V. A. ENGEL-LIEVENS

TWO HUNDRED THOUSAND DEAD GERMANS
ARE LISTED OUTSIDE THE BERLIN RED CROSS BUILDING

AN ARMY WITH BANNERS

SHRAPNEL

THE FRENCH LOWER THE AGE OF CONSENT

MOROCCO TO FRANCE TO GERMANY

SENEGALESE AND SOUVENIRS

A ZEPPELIN FALLS

"SPURLOS VERSENKT"

"TELL YOUR CAPTAIN TO COME ABOARD"

POLICE NOTICE
TAKE COVER

"THE ZEPPELINS ARE COMING!"

CLEOPATRA'S NEEDLE — LONDON

"WE BOMBED THE FORTRESS OF LONDON SUCCESSFULLY"

"BEYOND THE ALPS
LIES INFANTRY"

LONG RANGE GUN

THE ITALIANS ADVANCE

PANORAMA IN FLANDERS

LAND MINE

". . . ONLY THE MONSTROUS ANGER OF THE GUNS"

We're both needed to serve the Guns!
500
MEN
WANTED
JOIN THE
10th
QUEEN'S
TOWN HALL

"WHO'LL AVENGE NURSE CAVELL?"

KING AND COUNTRY

NATION OF SHOPKEEPERS

"IF I SHOULD DIE THINK ONLY THIS OF ME . . ."

CANADIANS AT VIMY: THE MAN AT THE LEFT HAS JUST BEEN STRUCK

". . . SHORT DAYS AGO
WE LIVED, FELT DAWN, SAW SUNSET GLOW . . ."

"FIRST AID!"

GERMAN CARTOON

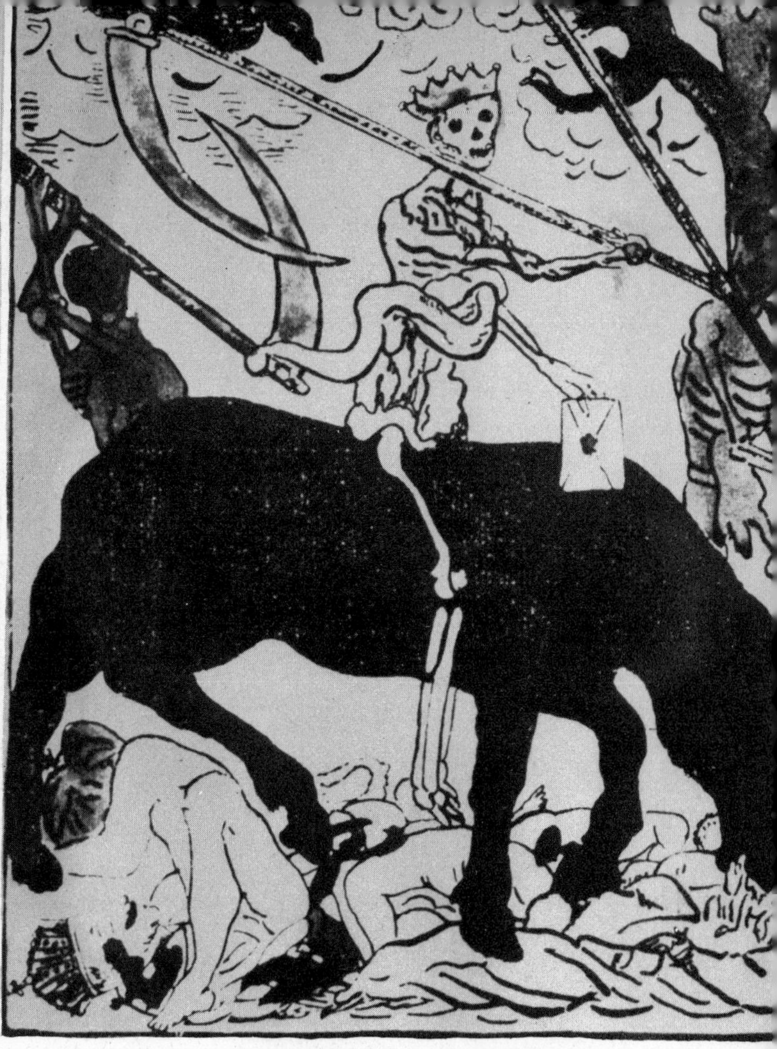

RUSSIAN CARTOON

DUTCH CARTOON

ITALIAN CARTOON

THEY SHALL
NOT PASS
VERDUN

WINGS OVER RHEIMS

"IS THERE NO PITY SITTING IN THE CLOUDS?"

". . . THE HALT AND THE BLIND . . ."

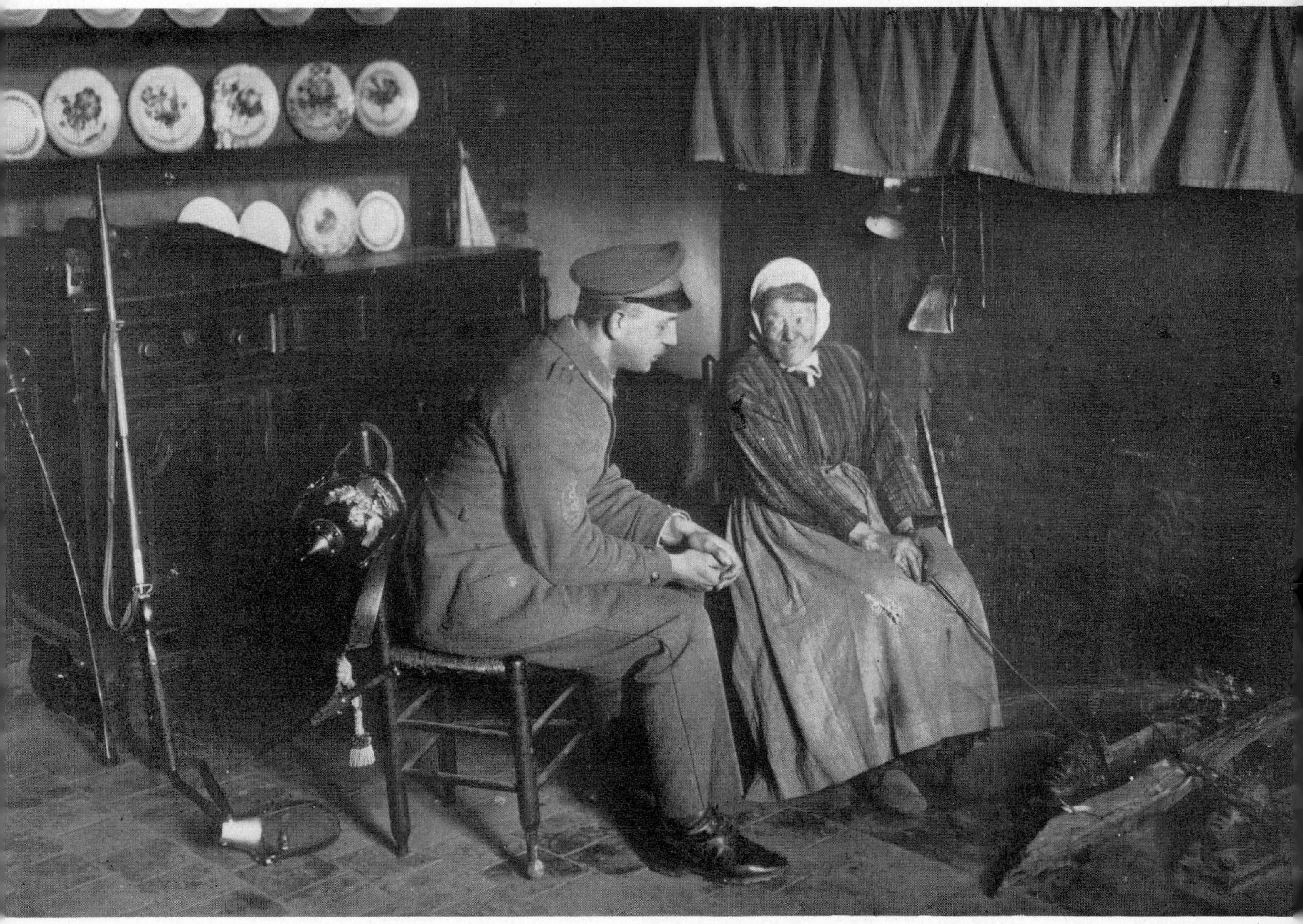

"C'EST LA GUERRE; COMME A LÀ GUERRE"

BLACK BREAD

"ANY CONTRABAND?"

AID AND COMFORT TO THE ENEMY

THE BRITISH KEEP A SECRET

PLUMES

IM WESTEN NICHTS NEUES

NO MORE PARADES

"... WHEN CITIES DECK THEIR STREETS FOR BARREN WARS WHICH HAVE LAID WASTE THEIR YOUTH ..."

MALNUTRITION

FOOD

Tauscht das Gold in Papiergeld um!

THE ALCHEMISTS

Helft uns siegen!
zeichnet
Kriegsanleihe

Pour la France
VERSEZ VOTRE OR
LIBERTÉ · ÉGALITÉ · FRATERNITÉ
1915
L'Or Combat Pour La Victoire

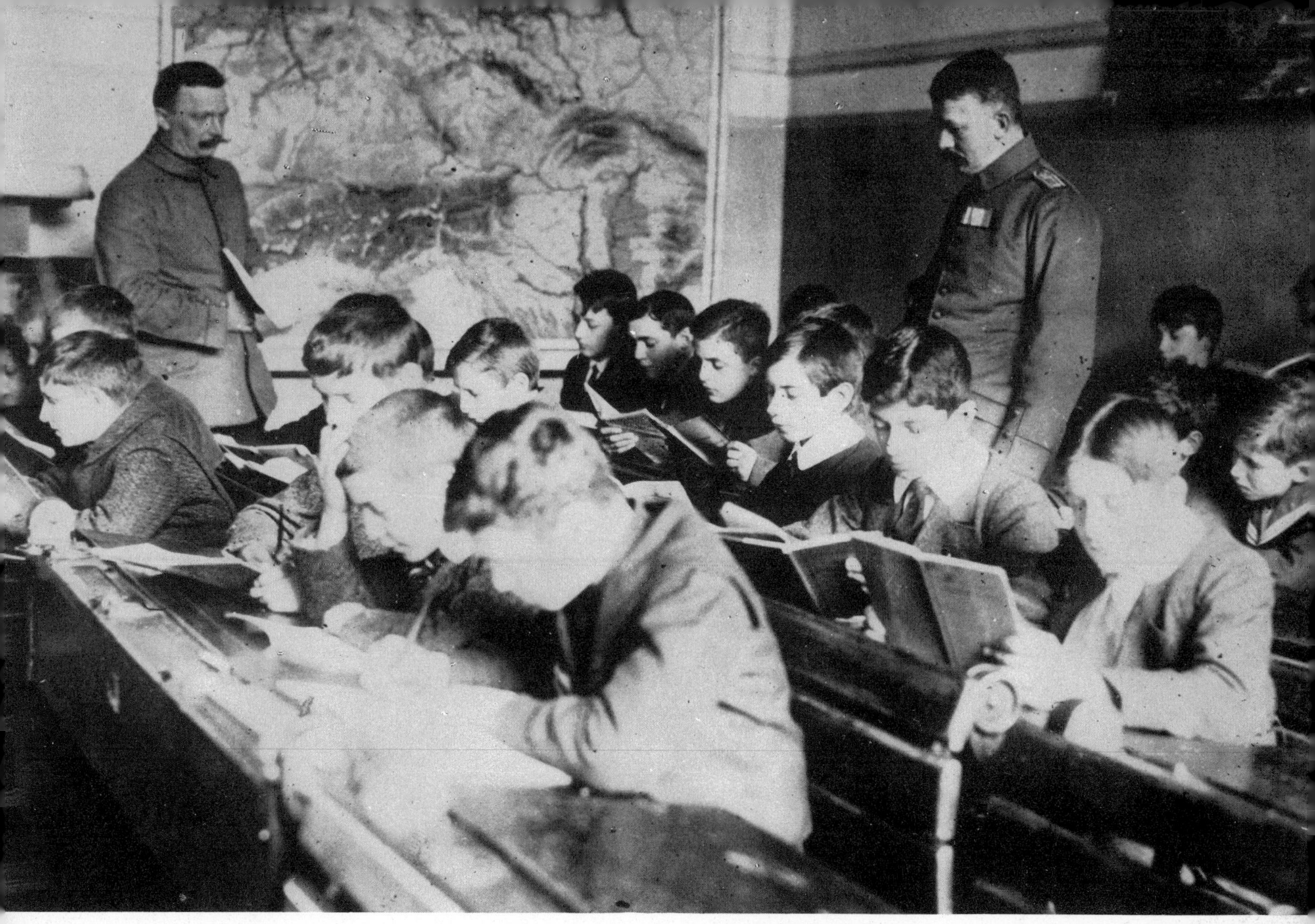

LORRAINE: *ICH BIN; DU BIST; ER IST*

ALSACE: IRREGULAR VERBS

ENNUI

". . . NO TRUCE WITH TIME, NOR TIME'S ACCOMPLICE, DEATH . . ."

DESERT SONG

GALLIPOLI

THE GARDEN OF EDEN

"FORTY CENTURIES ARE LOOKING DOWN UPON YOU!"

HINDENBURG LINE . . .

NORTH SEA TO THE VOSGES

CROSSROADS

CONCRETE

ANTI-TANK GUN, GERMAN MAKE

SECOND WAVE AT ARRAS

LANDMARK

LONDON TO BAGDAD

LANDING AT GALLIPOLI

"... JERUSALEM, JERUSALEM ..."

TAGS

ITALIA IRRIDENTA

"THERE IS NEITHER EAST NOR WEST"

ANTI-AIRCRAFT

A SPARROW FALLS

JULES FORTIN & Cie
ARRE
CAN RED C

"... SOME CORNER OF A FOREIGN FIELD THAT IS FOREVER ENGLAND"

FIRST WAVE: BULGARIANS

"ALLAH IL ALLAH DIN DIN DIN"

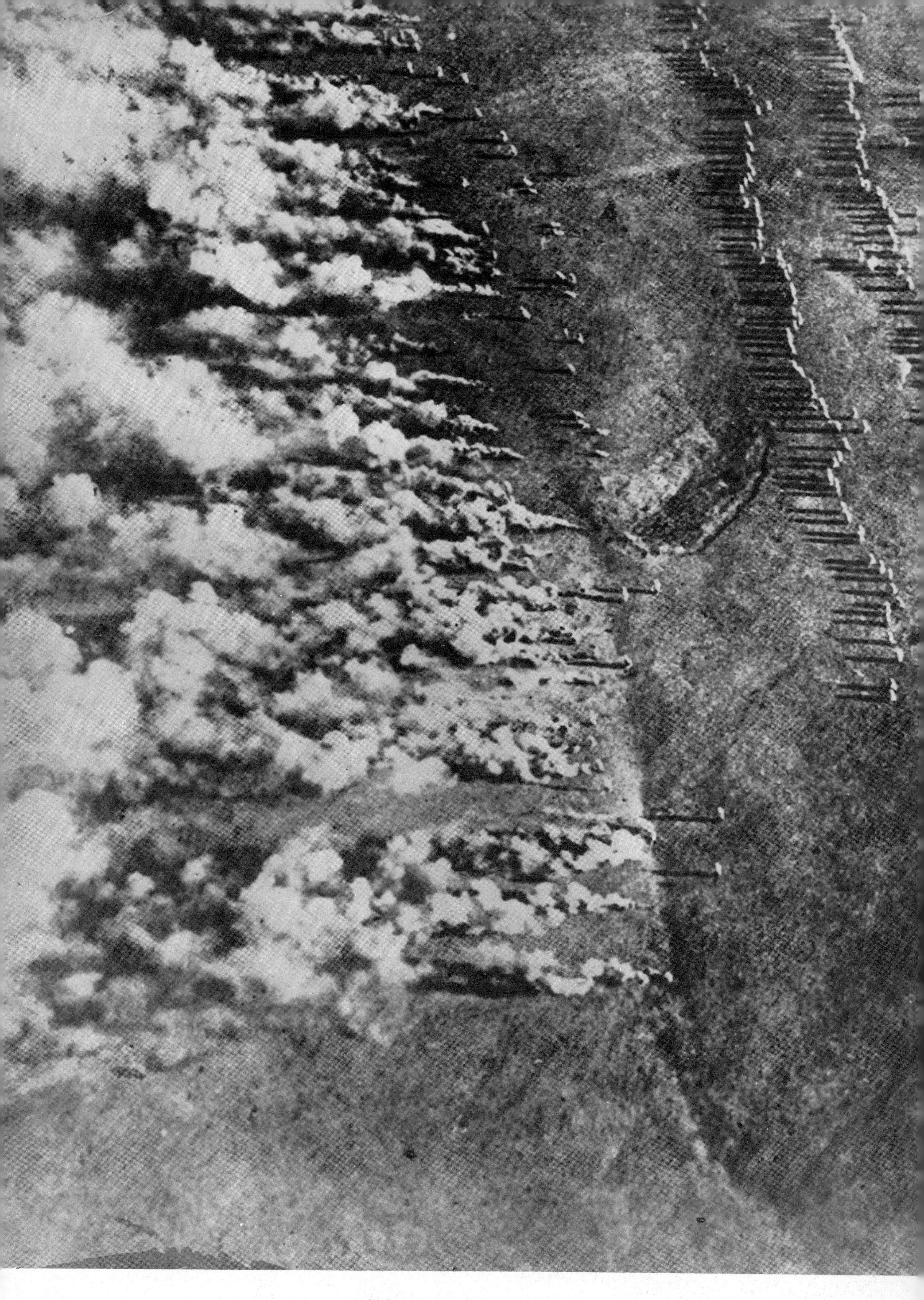

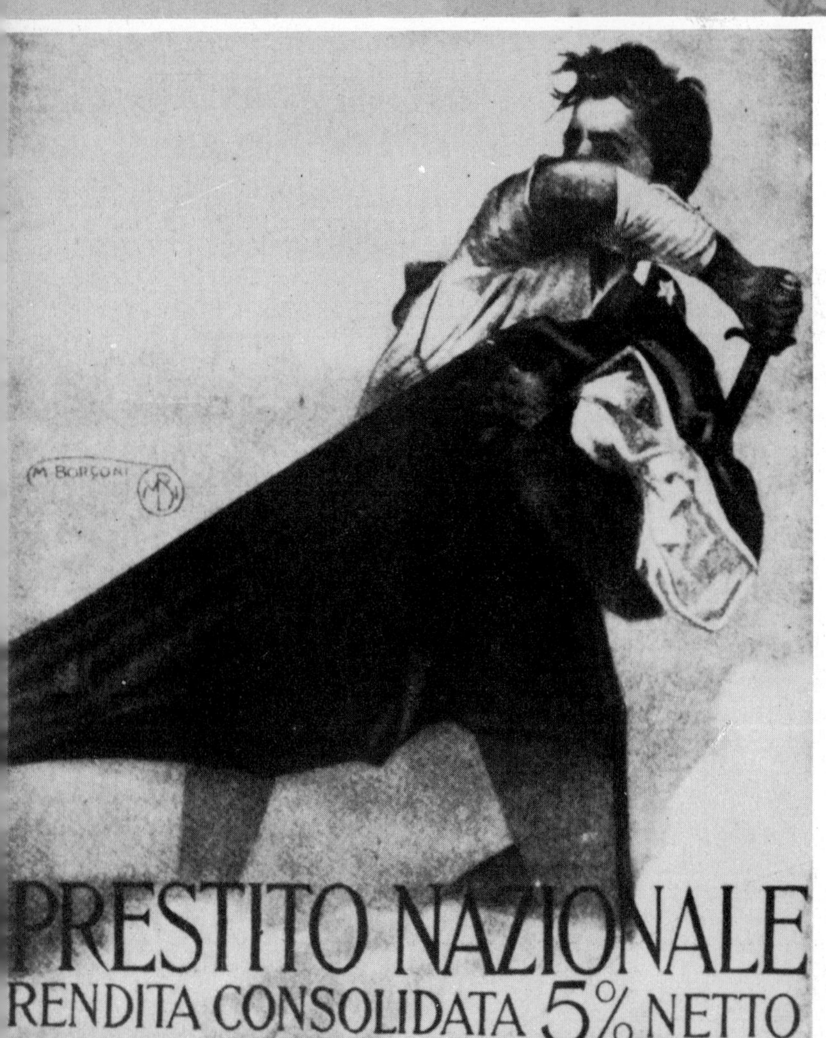
M. BORGONI
PRESTITO NAZIONALE
RENDITA CONSOLIDATA 5% NETTO
EMESSA A L.86,50 PER 100 NOMINALI
REDDITO EFFETTIVO 5,78% - ESENTE DA IMPOSTE PRESENTI E FUTURE.
LE SOTTOSCRIZIONI SI RICEVONO DAL 15 GENNAIO AL 3 FEBBRAIO
PRESSO TUTTE LE FILIALI DEGLI ISTITUTI DI EMISSIONE E PRESSO GLI ISTITUTI DI CREDITO ORDINARIO, LE CASSE DI RISPARMIO, LE BANCHE POPOLARI E COOPERATIVE, LE DITTE E SOCIETÀ BANCARIE PARTECIPANTI AL CONSORZIO PER L'EMISSIONE DEL PRESTITO.

NATIONAL SERVICE
WOMEN'S
LAND ARMY
"GOD SPEED THE PLOUGH
AND THE WOMAN WHO DRIVES IT"

BACKWASH: SERBIA TO ALBANIA

DEFENSE OF THE REALM ACT

THE
BRITISHERS' PROTECTION
TO SECURE THE
INTERNMENT OR DEPORTATION
OF ALL ALIEN ENEMIES
MALE & FEMALE
NATURALISED OR OTHERWISE
COME IN THOUSANDS
FALL IN ROYAL EXCHANGE STEPS
THURSDAY MAY 13TH 1915
NOON
MEETING
THERE IS STILL
FOR
YOU
THIS SPACE
FOR
A
FIT
MAN
Will you fill it?

SKY-LINE

THIRD WAVE AT ARRAS

OH GOD OUR HELP IN AGES PAST

OH GOD OUR HELP IN AGES PAST

OH GOD OUR HELP IN AGES PAST

"EINE KUGEL KAM GEFLOGEN"

"EINS, ZWEI, DREI, VIER"

A PLACE IN THE SUN

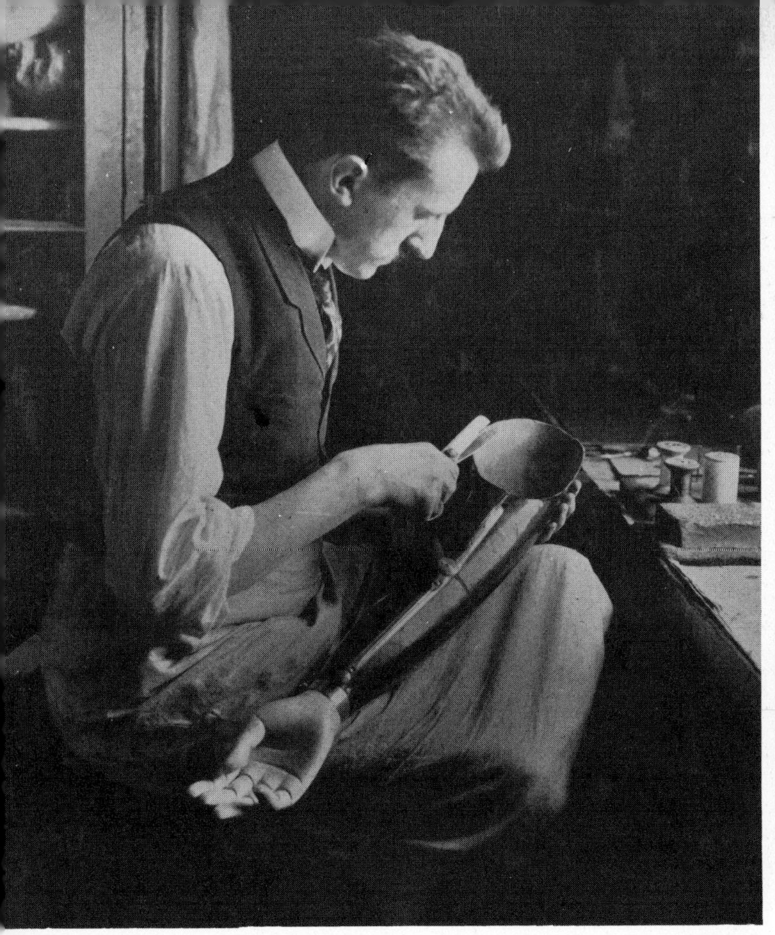

SUPPLY . . .

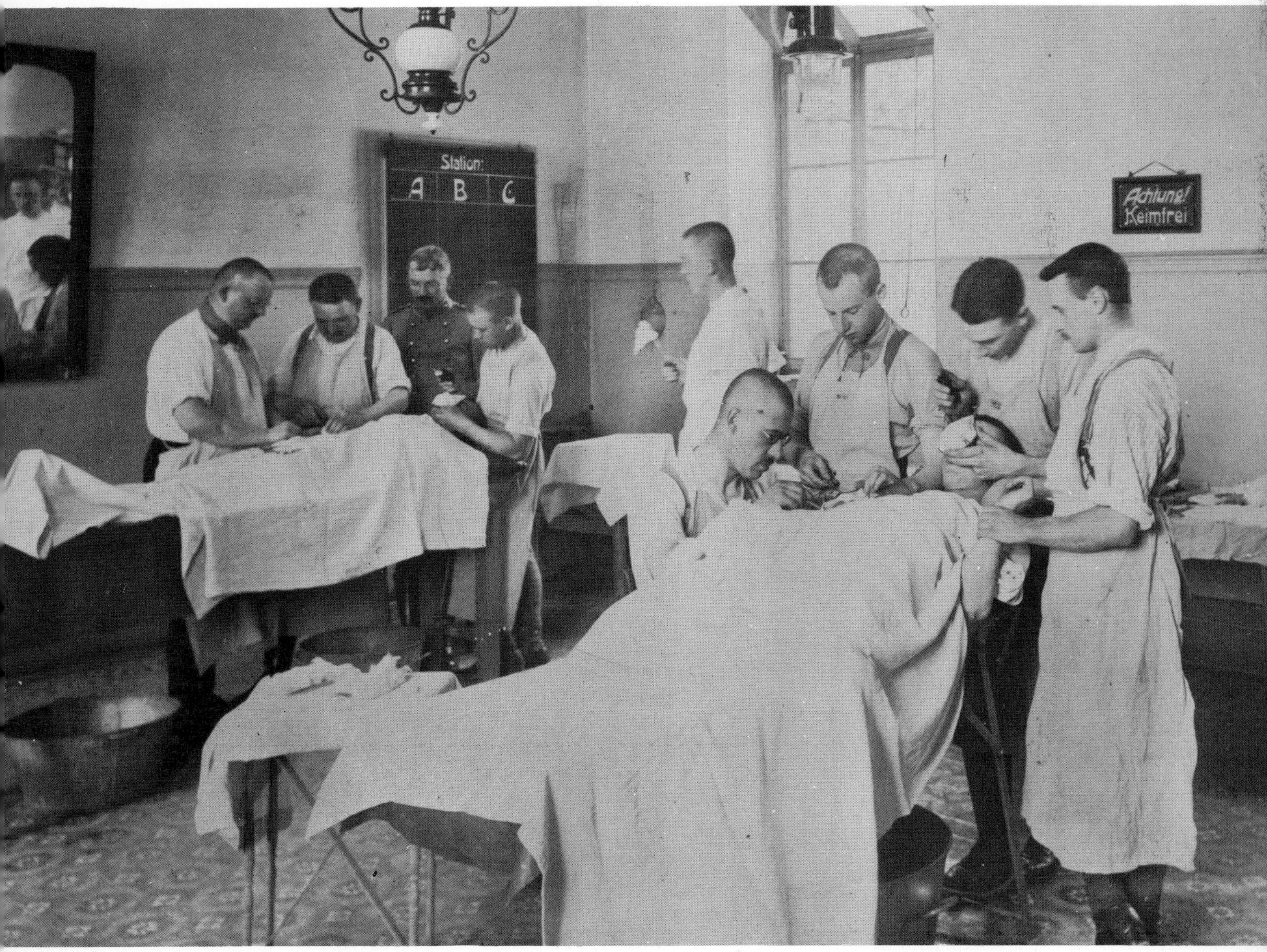

. . . DEMAND

CONTACT

ANTI-CONSCRIPTION IN LONDON

RUSSIAN WOMEN

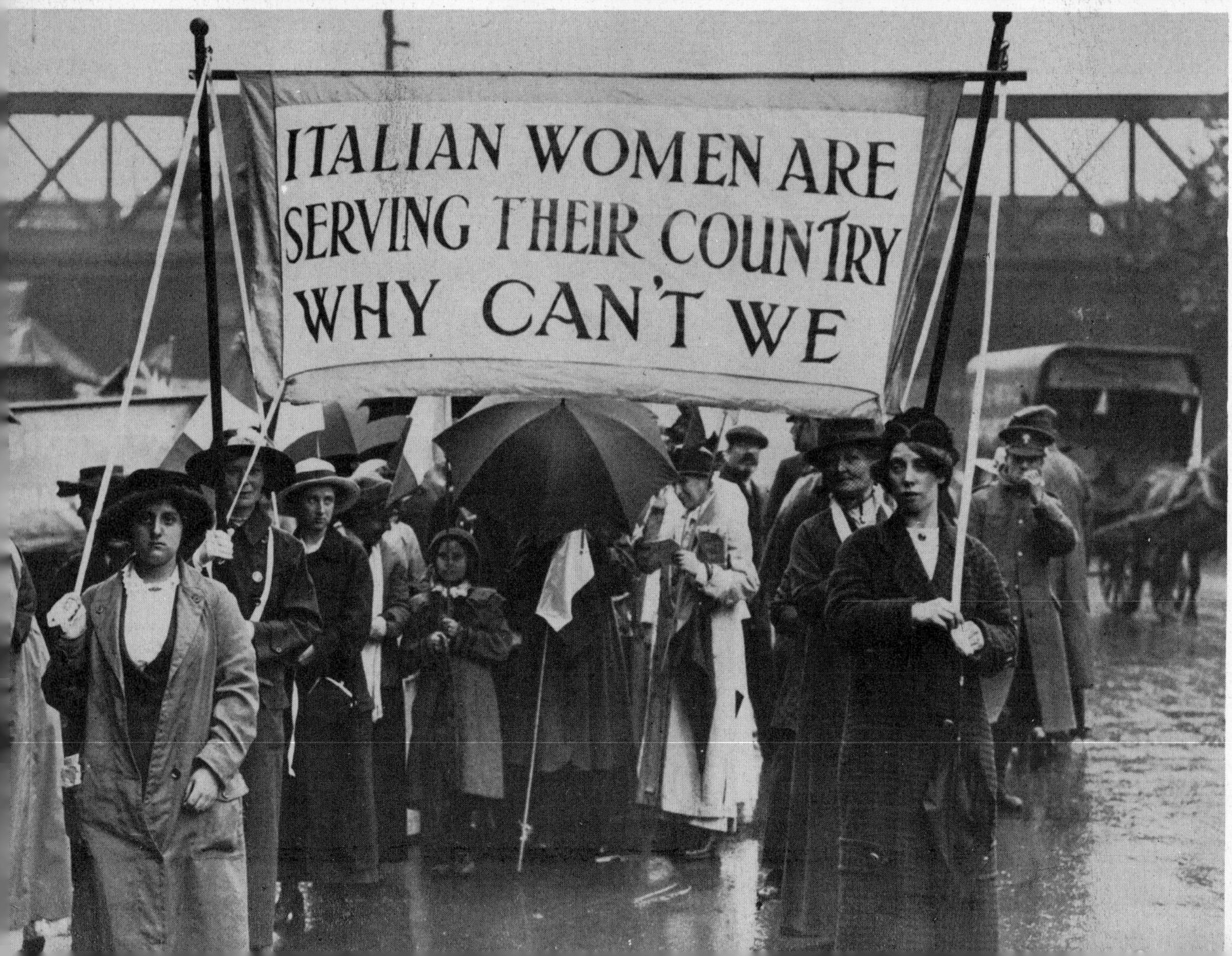

ENGLISH WOMEN

OUR
ROLL
OF HONOUR
IN THE GREAT WAR
PROUDLY
FLYING
THE
RIGHT
QUICKLY

CAMOUFLAGE

WIRE

"STABBING WITH PRACTICED MELANCHOLY, THIS BRIGHT, UNCOMPREHENDING WORLD"

FROM DOWN UNDER

MUTILÉS DE LA GUERRE

ORIENT EXPRESS

LOCAL COLOR

Canada!
Bernard Partridge

FRANKREICH
BELGIEN

Gott strafe England!
Simplicissimus-Verlag, München

The Sandwich Man
PEACE
ON EARTH
GOODWILL
TOWARD
MEN
WAR
AMMUNITION
FOR $ALE
ORDERS
FILLED
PROMPTLY
CULVER

WEATHER

Generally fair to-day and to-morrow; warmer to-day, colder by to-morrow night. Strong west winds

Full Report on Page 9

New York Tribune

First to Last—the Truth: News · Editorials · Advertisements

CIRCULATION
Over 100,000 Daily
Net Paid, Non-Returnable

Vol. LXXVI No. 25,648 | SUNDAY, FEBRUARY 4, 1917—SIX PARTS—SIXTY PAGES | PRICE FIVE CENTS

STATE GUARD CALLED AFTER MAYOR'S PLEA

Whitman Orders Out Land Forces and Naval Militia

CITY PROTECTED FROM TERRORISTS

Mitchel Confers with O'Ryan—11,000 Police on Defence Duty

Governor Whitman ordered the mobilization of the National Guard last night.

This step—to guard against possible acts of violence—was taken after a conference with Mayor Mitchel, Major General John F. O'Ryan, Adjutant General Stotesbury and Commissioner Robert P. Forshew, of the Naval Militia, at the Hotel St. Regis.

The Guard will be used to suppress any disorder that may occur and to protect the watersheds, armories, arsenals, aqueducts and bridges of the state against possible damage.

Fear of Terrorism

How much this is feared may be judged from the fact that although 11,000 police—all trained soldiers—are on guard in New York City, [illegible]

HEAR WILSON ASKED ALL NEUTRALS' AID

Washington, Feb. 3.—It was reported to-night in diplomatic quarters, but unconfirmed in any American official source, that President Wilson in advising neutrals of his action in severing diplomatic relations with Germany had invited other neutrals to follow his course.

AMERICAN SHIP U-BOAT VICTIM

Destruction of Housatonic May Be Basis of War Declaration

[From The Tribune Bureau]

Washington, Feb. 3.—The gravest concern was felt by State Department officials to-night when they received news from London of the sinking by a submarine of the American steamship Housatonic. It was realized that this might be the necessary overt act which would cause war.

It was said, however, that the Housatonic case would not be considered by this government until the evidence was all in. If the ship was sunk without warning it presents a casus belli, otherwise not.

According to the dispatches from London, the ship was sunk by a German submarine about noon to-day, when she was off the Scilly Islands. It is reported in London that no warning was given, but this has not been verified. All the officers and crew were saved by a British armed steamer.

Wilson's Warning

STANDING BACK OF HIM

Wilson Breaks With Germany; War Imminent

Bernstorff Dismissed, Gerard Recalled; "Overt Act," Sacrificing American Lives or Ships, Means Fight, Is President's Warning

HOSTILITIES MAY BE FORCED ON THIS NATION IN NEXT 48 HOURS

Officials Close to Executive Believe Armed Clash Is Inevitable—Appropriation for Conflict May Be Introduced To-morrow—President Declares He'll Use "Any Means Necessary" to Protect Seamen and Citizens on the High Seas

By STEVENSON H. EVANS

Washington, Feb. 3.—War is now as near as one second is to another. Only a miracle can prevent the taking of the next step, which means the beginning of actual hostilities against the Germans.

STAFF WORK: CAVIAR TO THE GENERAL

TACTICAL BLUNDER

HARASSING FIRE

THIS WAS A HOME

THIS WAS A CHURCH

THIS WAS A FOREST

THIS WAS A MAN

MARCH SLAV

"TOVARISTCH!"

"All the News That's Fit to Print."

The New York Times.

THE WEATHER

VOL. LXVI ... NO. 21,602. NEW YORK, SATURDAY, MARCH 17, 1917.—TWENTY PAGES.

THE ROMANOFF DYNASTY ENDED IN RUSSIA; CZAR'S ABDICATION FOLLOWED BY MICHAEL'S; CONSTITUTIONAL ASSEMBLY TO BE CONVOKED

New Russian Government Asks People's Support;

"THE MASSES TAKE FORCIBLE CHARGE OF THEIR OWN DESTINY"

HIGH COMMAND

NEW DRAFT

GIRLS

JOURNEY'S END

WAITING LIST

HUNGER

BIG BERTHA

FRIEND OR ENEMY?

"ANT HEAP"

"All the News That's Fit to Print."

The New York Times.

THE WEATHER

VOL. LXVI...NO. 21,633. NEW YORK, TUESDAY, APRIL 17, 1917.—TWENTY PAGES.

FRENCH PIERCE 25-MILE FRONT, TAKE 10,000 PRISONERS; BRITISH IN SEVEN DAYS HAVE SMASHED 10 GERMAN DIVISIONS; GREAT GENERAL OFFENSIVE OPENS; STRIKES BEGIN IN BERLIN

Offensive Now Under Way Along the Whole Line;

NEW YORK JOURNAL

EIGHTH EDITION

House by a Vote of 373 to 50 Passes Joint Resolution

WAR IS DECLARED BY U.S.

The New York Times.

"All the News That's Fit to Print."

THE WEATHER

PRESIDENT PROCLAIMS WAR; WARNS ALIEN ENEMIES HERE; 91 GERMAN SHIPS SEIZED AND SPIES PUT UNDER ARREST; NAVY MOBILIZED AT ONCE; CUBA AND BRAZIL MAY JOIN US

27 SHIPS TAKEN HERE

Government May Use Liners Later as Troop Transports.

Bryan Asks the President to Enroll Him as a Private

MENOCAL DEMANDS WAR

President Urges Congress to Authorize Action; No Opposition Expected.

Think German Kaiser Vetoed Peace Proposal by Austria

WHOLESALE PLOT ARRESTS

Sixty German Suspects in New York and Other Cities Locked Up.

President's Proclamation of a State of War, and Regulations Governing Alien Enemies

A PROCLAMATION.

GOVERNMENT ACTS SWIFTLY

War Tidings Fly to Navy and Army When Wilson Signs Resolution.

New York American

WAR WITH GERMANY

Sixty-fifth Congress of the United States of America;

At the First Session,

Begun and held at the City of Washington on Monday, the second day of April, one thousand nine hundred and seventeen.

JOINT RESOLUTION

Declaring that a state of war exists between the Imperial German Government and the Government and the people of the United States and making provision to prosecute the same.

Whereas the Imperial German Government has committed repeated acts of war against the Government and the people of the United States of America: Therefore be it

Resolved by the Senate and House of Representatives of the United States of America in Congress assembled, That the state of war between the United States and the Imperial German Government which has thus been thrust upon the United States is hereby formally declared; and that the President be, and he is hereby, authorized and directed to employ the entire naval and military forces of the United States and the resources of the Government to carry on war against the Imperial German Government; and to bring the conflict to a successful termination all of the resources of the country are hereby pledged by the Congress of the United States.

Champ Clark,

Speaker of the House of Representatives.

Thos. R. Marshall

Vice President of the United States and President of the Senate.

Approved 6 April, 1917

Woodrow Wilson

". . . A SCARRED SLOPE OF BATTERED HILL"

ENTANGLEMENTS

ZERO HOUR

WOODS

FOLLOW THE FLAG

ENLIST IN THE NAVY

I WANT YOU FOR U.S. ARMY

NEAREST RECRUITING STATION

FILL THE BREECH

THE NAVY NEEDS YOU! DON'T READ AMERICAN HISTORY— MAKE IT!

COLUMBIA CALLS

ENLIST NOW FOR U.S. ARMY

THINK!

ARE YOU CONTENT FOR HIM TO FIGHT FOR **YOU**?

WON'T YOU DO YOUR BIT?

WE SHALL WIN BUT **YOU** MUST HELP

JOIN TO-DAY

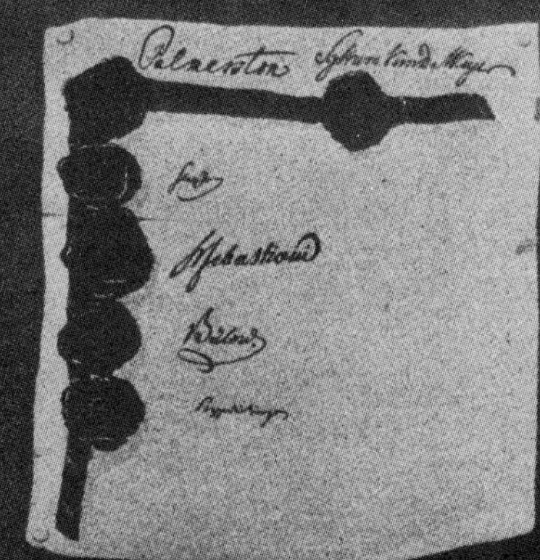

These are the signatures and seals of the representatives of the Six Powers to the Scrap of Paper—the Treaty signed in 1839 guaranteeing the independence and neutrality of Belgium.
"Palmerston" signed for Britain, "Bulow" for Prussia

The Germans have broken their pledged word and devastated Belgium. Help to keep your Country's honour bright by restoring Belgium her liberty

ENLIST TO-DAY

GET INTO THE FIGHT · BUY LIBERTY BONDS
BUY

PRACTICE

"YOU'RE IN THE ARMY NOW, YOU'RE NOT BEHIND THE PLOW . . ."

INSPECTION

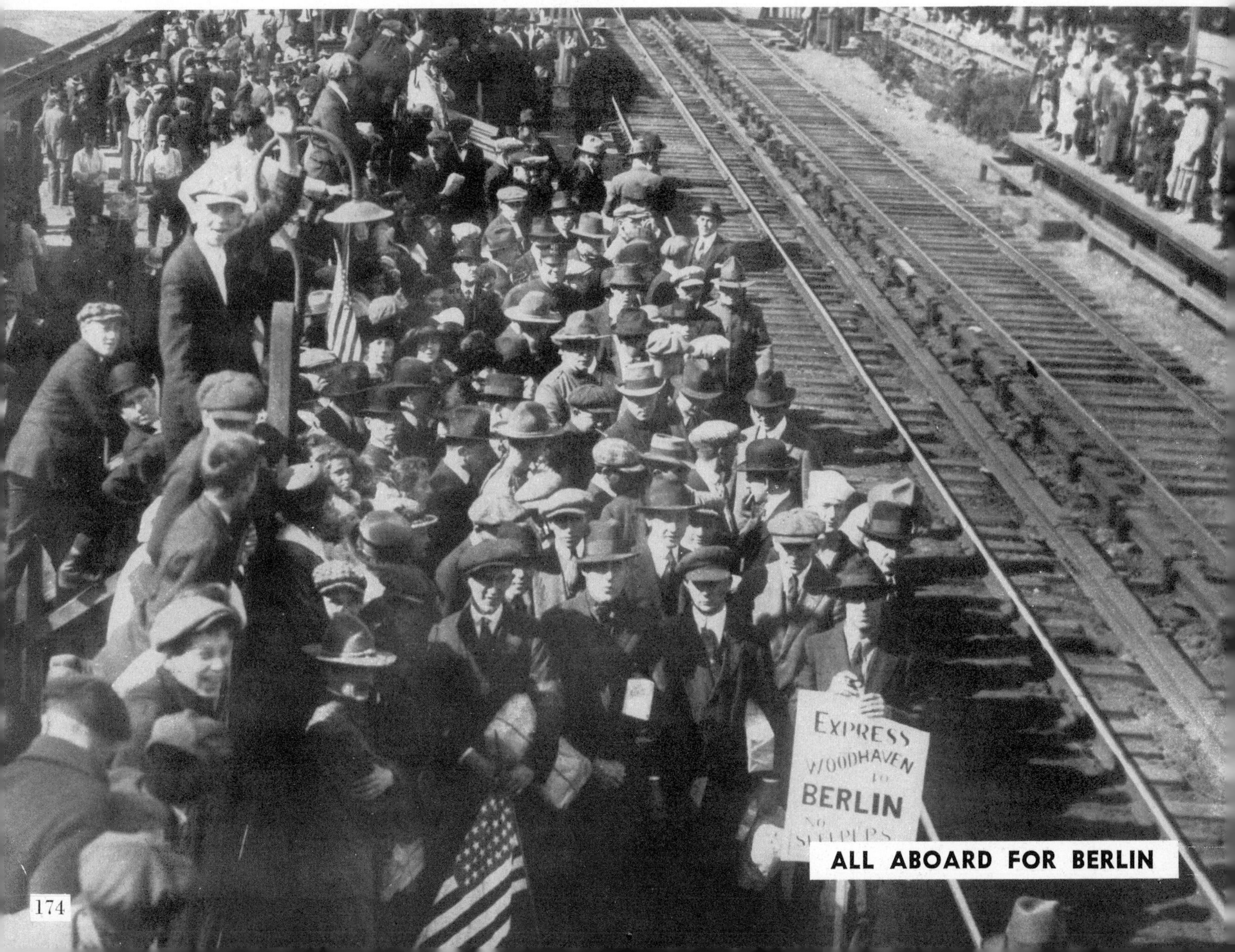

ALL ABOARD FOR BERLIN

"All the News That's Fit to Print."

The New York Times.

THE WEATHER

VOL. LXVI...NO. 21,665. NEW YORK, SATURDAY, MAY 19, 1917.—TWENTY PAGES.

PRESIDENT CALLS THE NATION TO ARMS; DRAFT BILL SIGNED; REGISTRATION ON JUNE 5; REGULARS UNDER PERSHING TO GO TO FRANCE

WILL NOT SEND ROOSEVELT

Wilson Not to Avail Himself of Volunteer ...

A Proclamation by the President of the United States

Executive Mansion, Washington, D. C., May 18, 1917.

PLANS FOR NATIONAL ARMY

First Draft of 500,000

STEEL COMMON SOARS
IN MILLION-SHARE DAY

Gains 4 1-4 Points to 107 1-4, a New High Record for Year,

OVERTIME

"...THE YANKS ARE COMING..."

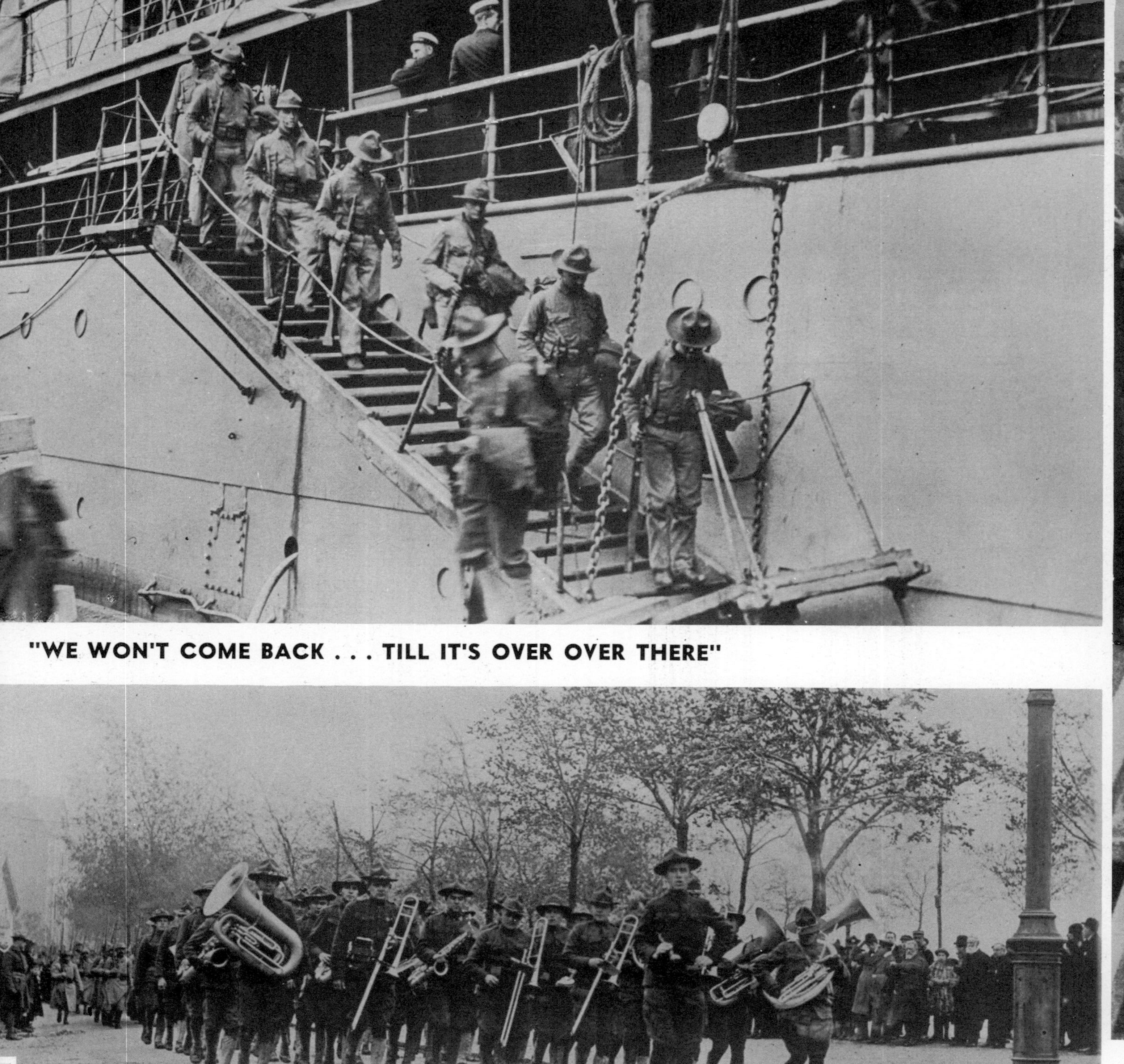

"WE WON'T COME BACK . . . TILL IT'S OVER OVER THERE"

"NOUS VOILÀ, LAFAYETTE!"

ENEMY ALIENS

IMPRESSIONS

COLLECTING STATION

BABE IN THE WOODS

"IT'S A LONG WAY TO TIPPERARY . . ."

FRANCE

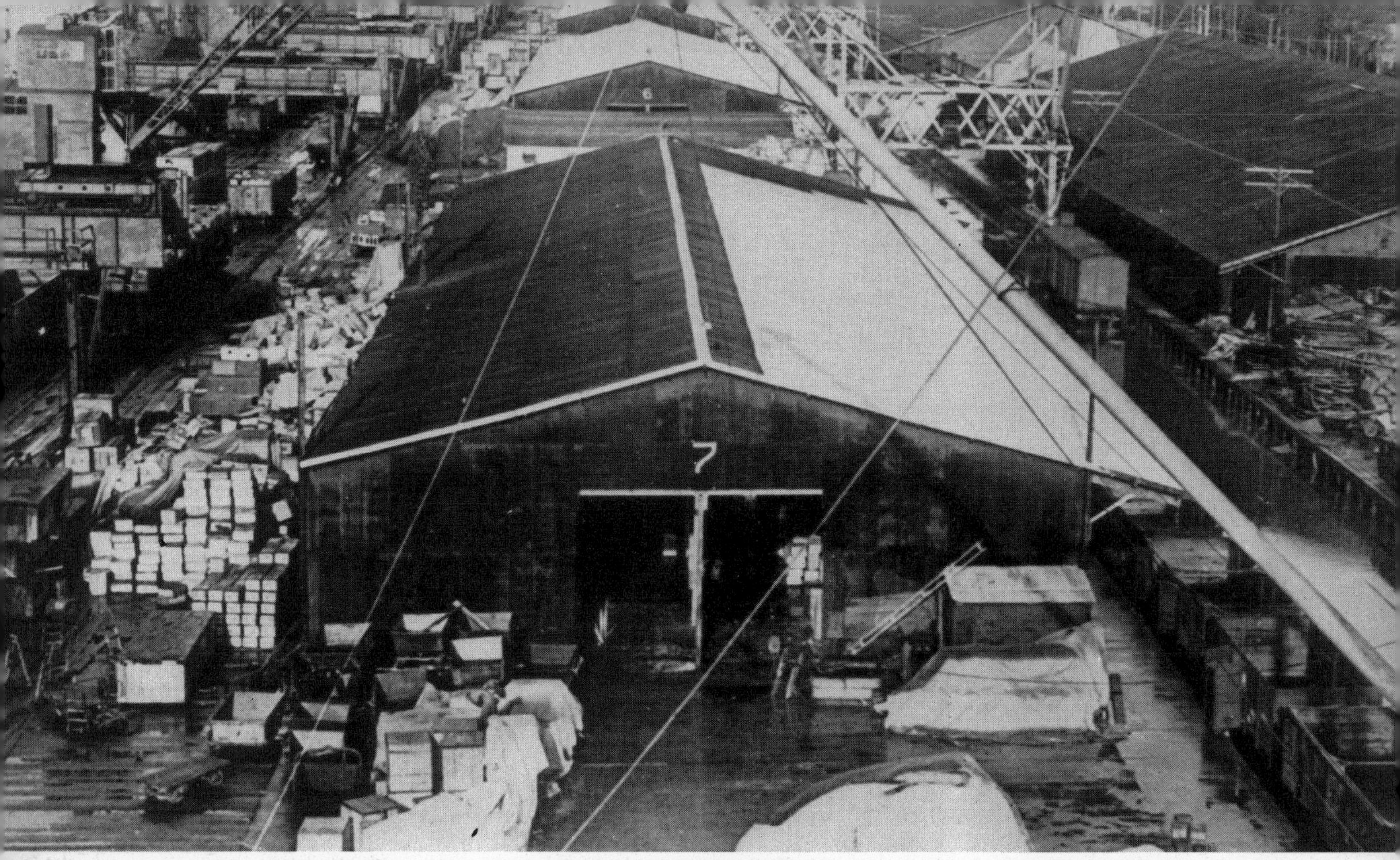

"CHOW!"

CONSUMERS LEAGUE
of
Brownsville
& EAST NEW YORK
IN THE NAME
OF BROWNSVILLE
WE
PROTEST
AGAINST
THE HIGH COST
OF
LIVING

TRANSPORT

SURVIVORS

STREET SCENE

HURDLES

PASTORAL

HANDS ACROSS THE SEA

CREDIT COMMERCIAL DE FRANCE
SOUSCRIVEZ POUR LA VICTOIRE ET LA LIBERTE
ENTREE
ENTRANCE

PATROL

SUPPORT

OUTPOST

DEATH IN THE AFTERNOON

"KAMERAD!"

FIELD GUN, UNATTENDED

CAPTURE IN NO MAN'S LAND

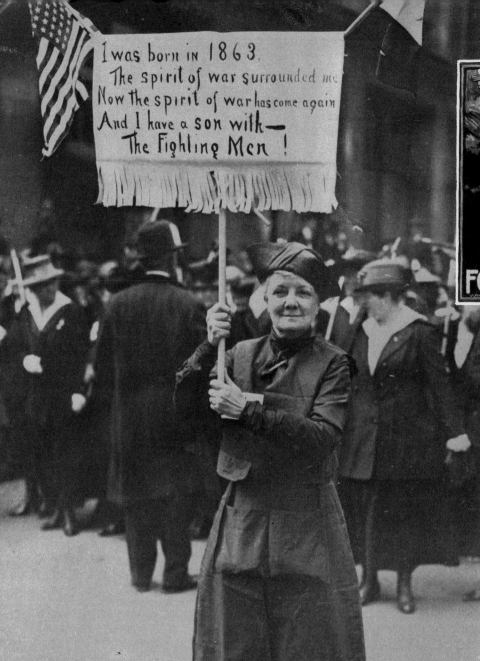

I was born in 1863.
The spirit of war surrounded me
Now the spirit of war has come again
And I have a son with—
The Fighting Men!

FOR VICTORY, BUY BONDS

Lend
the way they
Fight
Buy Bonds
to your UTMOST

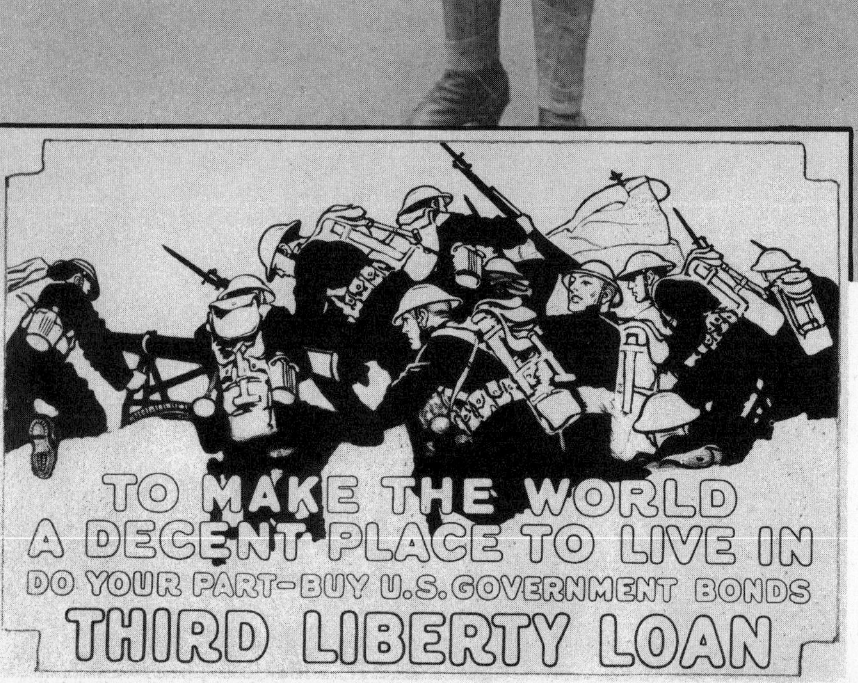
TO MAKE THE WORLD
A DECENT PLACE TO LIVE IN
DO YOUR PART–BUY U.S. GOVERNMENT BONDS
THIRD LIBERTY LOAN

INTO THE JAWS OF DEATH

"KEEP YOUR HEAD DOWN, ALLEMAND"

OPEN COUNTRY

TERRAIN

TWO MINUTES TO GO

"COME OUT, COME OUT, WHEREVER YOU ARE"

IMPROVEMENTS

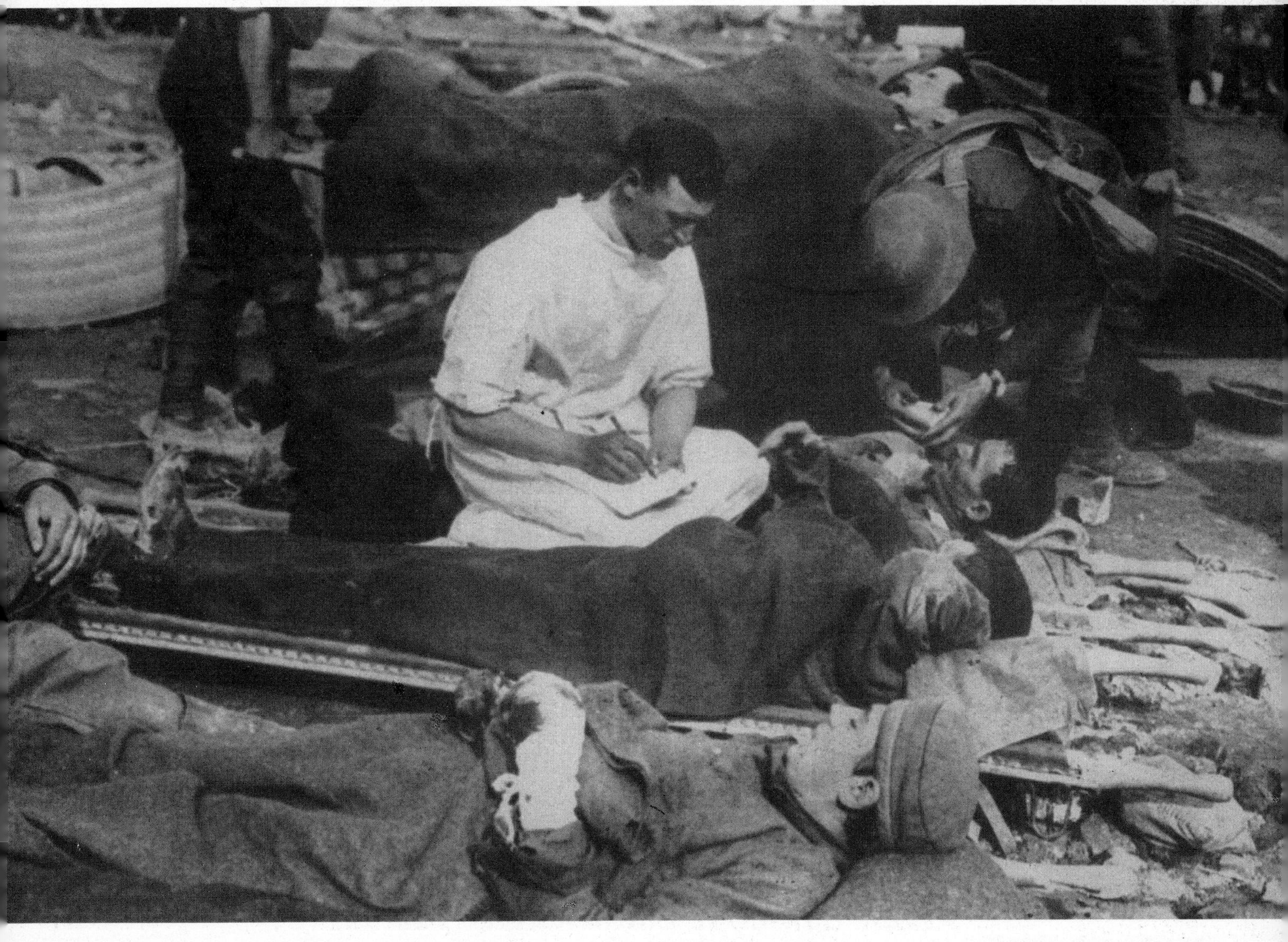

"NEXT OF KIN?"

KOLOSSAL!

PROJECTILE

ITALY: FAREWELL TO ARMS

SOMME: BRITISH ADVANCE

BARRAGE

"O, LITTLE TOWN OF BETHLEHEM"

ALLENBY ENTERS JERUSALEM

DERELICT

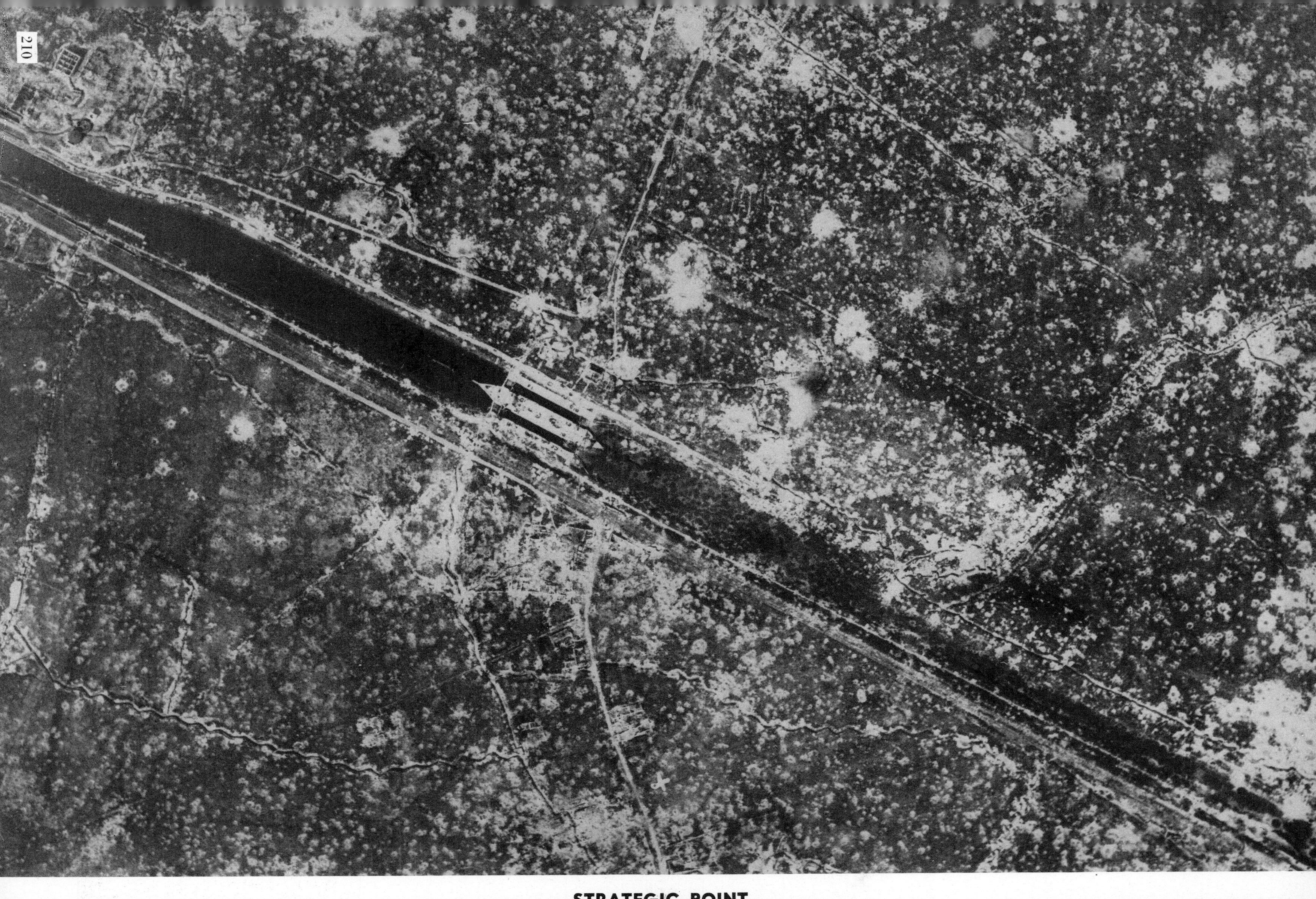

STRATEGIC POINT

DOG FIGHT

ACE

". . . AND NO BIRDS SING . . ."

FIRST ROUND — AMERICAN

FIELD OF HONOR

MADE IN GERMANY

New York American

GREATER NEW YORK EDITION — AN AMERICAN PAPER FOR THE AMERICAN PEOPLE — GREATER NEW YORK EDITION

TWO CENTS

No. 12,665. — FRIDAY, MARCH 22, 1918—22 PAGES — PRICE TWO CENTS

GREAT GERMAN DRIVE BEGINS; ATTACK HAIG ON 50-MILE FRONT

WHITMAN

Berlin Sends War Threat to Holland

ENGLAND CALM AS GREAT BATTLE IS RAGING; ALLIED SHIPS AND FLIERS FIGHT IN NORTH SEA

Section 1

"All the News That's Fit to Print."

The New York Times.

THE WEATHER

Section 1

NEW YORK, SUNDAY, MARCH 24, 1918. 108 PAGES. In Nine Parts. FIVE CENTS

GERMANS SMASH BRITISH FRONT, DRIVE IN FOUR MILES; CLAIM 25,000 PRISONERS; HELD AT SOME POINTS, SAYS HAIG; GUN SAID TO BE 74½ MILES AWAY LANDS SHELLS IN PARIS

FRENCH CAPITAL UNDER FIRE

Paris Reports That City is Shelled From a Distance of 74 Miles

SAYS BRITISH ARE BEATEN

Americans Capture German In His Own Listening Post

LINES HOLDING IN NORTH

Emperor Commands and Directs the Drive in Person; Crown Prince and Hindenburg With Him in Belgium

SPOILS

TORCH AND FLAME

SPECIAL ORDER OF THE DAY
By FIELD-MARSHAL SIR DOUGLAS HAIG
K.T., G.C.B., G.C.V.O., K.C.I.E
Commander-in-Chief, British Armies in France.

D. Haig. F.M.

To ALL RANKS OF THE BRITISH ARMY IN FRANCE AND FLANDERS.

Three weeks ago to-day the enemy began his terrific attacks against us on a fifty-mile front. His objects are to separate us from the French, to take the Channel Ports and destroy the British Army.

In spite of throwing already 106 Divisions into the battle and enduring the most reckless sacrifice of human life, he has as yet made little progress towards his goals.

We owe this to the determined fighting and self-sacrifice of our troops. Words fail me to express the admiration which I feel for the splendid resistance offered by all ranks of our Army under the most trying circumstances.

Many amongst us now are tired. To those I would say that Victory will belong to the side which holds out the longest. The French Army is moving rapidly and in great force to our support.

There is no other course open to us but to fight it out. Every position must be held to the last man: there must be no retirement. With our backs to the wall and believing in the justice of our cause each one of us must fight on to the end. The safety of our homes and the Freedom of mankind alike depend upon the conduct of each one of us at this critical moment.

D. Haig. F.M.

Commander-in-Chief,
British Armies in France.

General Headquarters,
Thursday, April 11th, 1918.

HARVEST

DETAIL

A GAP

FRENCH TRENCHES BECOME GERMAN TRENCHES

IT'S BILLIONS FOR DEFENSE, OR BILLIONS FOR INDEMNITY!

"All the News That's Fit to Print."

The New York Times.

THE WEATHER
Showers today; Thursday fair; light, variable winds.

VOL. LXVII. NO. 21,998. NEW YORK, WEDNESDAY, APRIL 17, 1918.—TWENTY-FOUR PAGES. TWO CENTS

GERMANS TAKE MOST OF MESSINES RIDGE AFTER SWEEPING HAIG OUT OF BAILLEUL; NOTHING VITAL LOST, SAYS LLOYD GEORGE

Section 1

"All the News That's Fit to Print."

The New York Times.

THE WEATHER
Fair Sunday; Monday partly cloudy; moderate south winds.

Section 1

VOL. LXVII...NO. 22,009. NEW YORK, SUNDAY, APRIL 28, 1918.—108 PAGES, In Nine Parts, FIVE CENTS

RUSSIANS REVOLT, NAME CZAREVITCH RULER; ALLIES HOLDING FAST ON KEMMEL FRONT; GERMANS HALT, AWAITING REINFORCEMENTS

". . . AND THREE WITH A NEW SONG'S MEASURE CAN TRAMPLE AN EMPIRE DOWN"

"All the News That's Fit to Print."

The New York Times.

THE WEATHER

GERMANS GET CHEMIN DES DAMES IN NEW DRIVE;
BLOW ON 40-MILE FRONT REACHES THE AISNE;
PAY DEARLY THERE; REPULSED IN FLANDERS

MASSE MENSCH

FRAGMENTS

ALL MERCHANDISE ADVERTISED IN THE TRIBUNE IS *GUARANTEED*

New York Tribune

First to Last — the Truth: News · Editorials · Advertisements

WEATHER
Fair to-day and to-morrow; warmer to-morrow; moderate shifting winds.
Full Report on Page 7

Vol. LXXVIII No. 26,162 — (Copyright 1918— The Tribune Ass'n) — WEDNESDAY, JULY 3, 1918 — TWO CENTS In Greater New York and commuting distance | THREE CENTS Elsewhere

Over 1,000,000 U. S. Soldiers Sent Abroad; Americans Drive On, Smash Counter Blows

RAID

"All the News That's Fit to Print."

The New York Times.

THE WEATHER

VOL. LXVII...NO. 22,088. NEW YORK, TUESDAY, JULY 16, 1918.—TWENTY-FOUR PAGES. TWO CENTS

AMERICANS DRIVE GERMANS BACK OVER MARNE; TAKE 1,000 PRISONERS AND CHECK BIG DRIVE; GERMAN ATTACK ON A 60-MILE FRONT FAILS

AMERICAN FORCE | Bombard Our Hospitals | FOCH SATISFIED WITH DAY | Official Reports of the Day's Operations | AMERICAN BLOW UPSETS FOE

CHATEAU-THIERRY

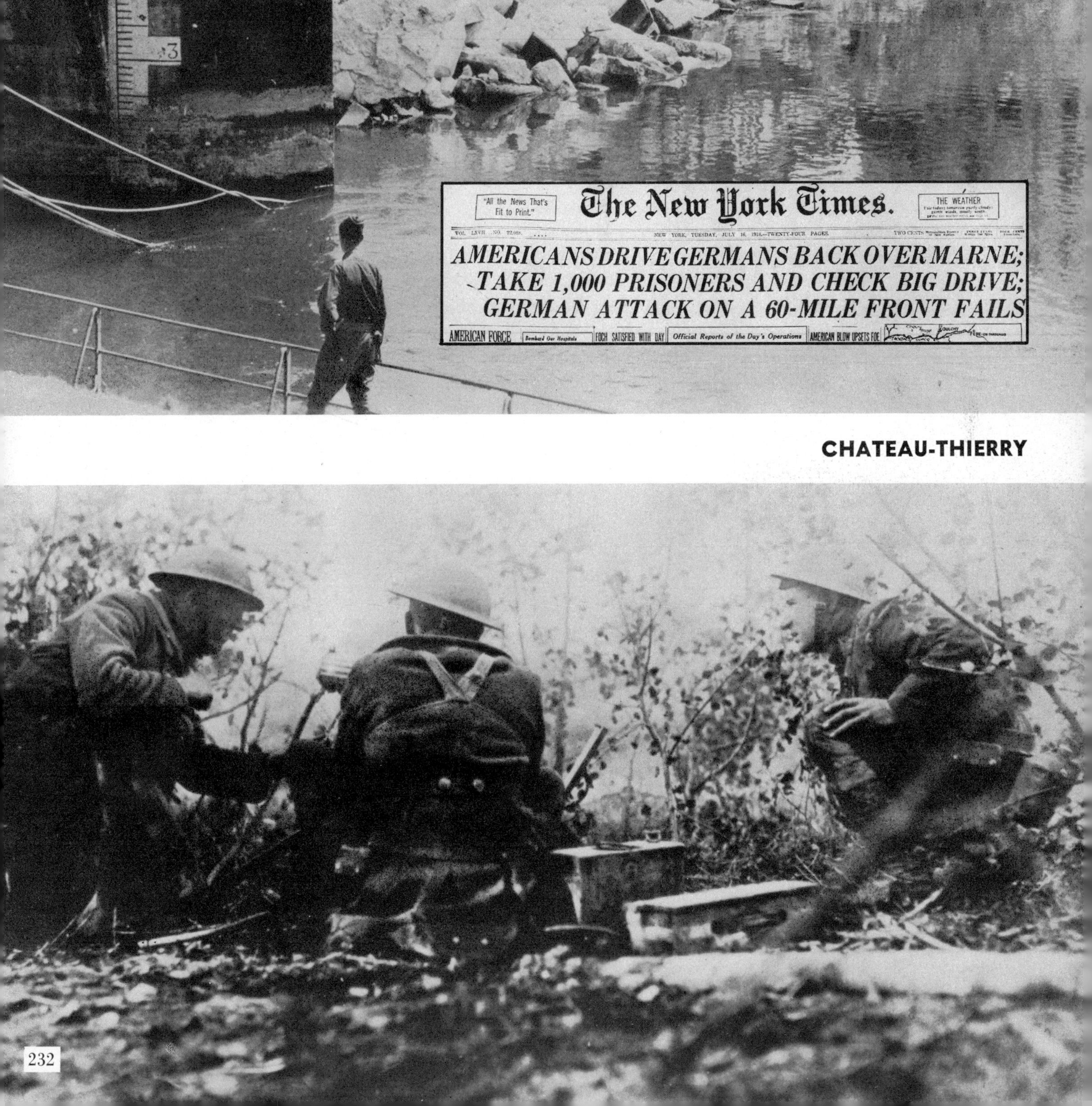

BULL'S-EYE

"I'VE BEEN WORKING ON THE RAILROAD"

MONTFAUCON

ST. QUENTIN

Section 1

"All the News That's Fit to Print."

The New York Times.

THE WEATHER

Section 1

VOL. LXVII...NO. 22,093. NEW YORK, SUNDAY, JULY 21, 1918.—92 PAGES, In Nine Parts, FIVE CENTS

ALL GERMANS PUSHED BACK OVER THE MARNE; ALLIES GAIN THREE MILES SOUTH OF SOISSONS; NOW HOLD 20,000 PRISONERS AND 400 GUNS

SAN DIEGO'S LOSS STILL UNEXPLAINED;

Moscow Now Attacked By Cholera Scourge

EX-CZAR OF RUSSIA KILLED BY ORDER

Germans Try to Excuse Retreat Over the Marne

FIERCE FIGHTING YESTERDAY

Our Men in a Severe

Official Reports of the Day's Operations

French

German

BERLIN ADMITS RETREAT

Says Troops Withdrew

"All the News That's Fit to Print."

The New York Times.

THE WEATHER

NEW YORK, FRIDAY, AUGUST 9, 1918.—TWENTY PAGES.

TWO CENTS

HAIG BREAKS FOE'S LINE ON 25-MILE FRONT; GAINS 7 MILES, TAKES 10,000 MEN, 100 GUNS; GERMAN MAN POWER VISIBLY ON THE WANE

URGES PRESIDENT | Bulgar King in Germany | FORMING 'LAST STAND' ARMY | "Tenacity, Audacity, Victory," Petain's Words to His Soldiers | BRITISH SURPRISE GERMANS | Official Reports of the Allied Successes | ATTACK BEGINS AT DAWN

SNIPERS

RETURN OF THE SOLDIER

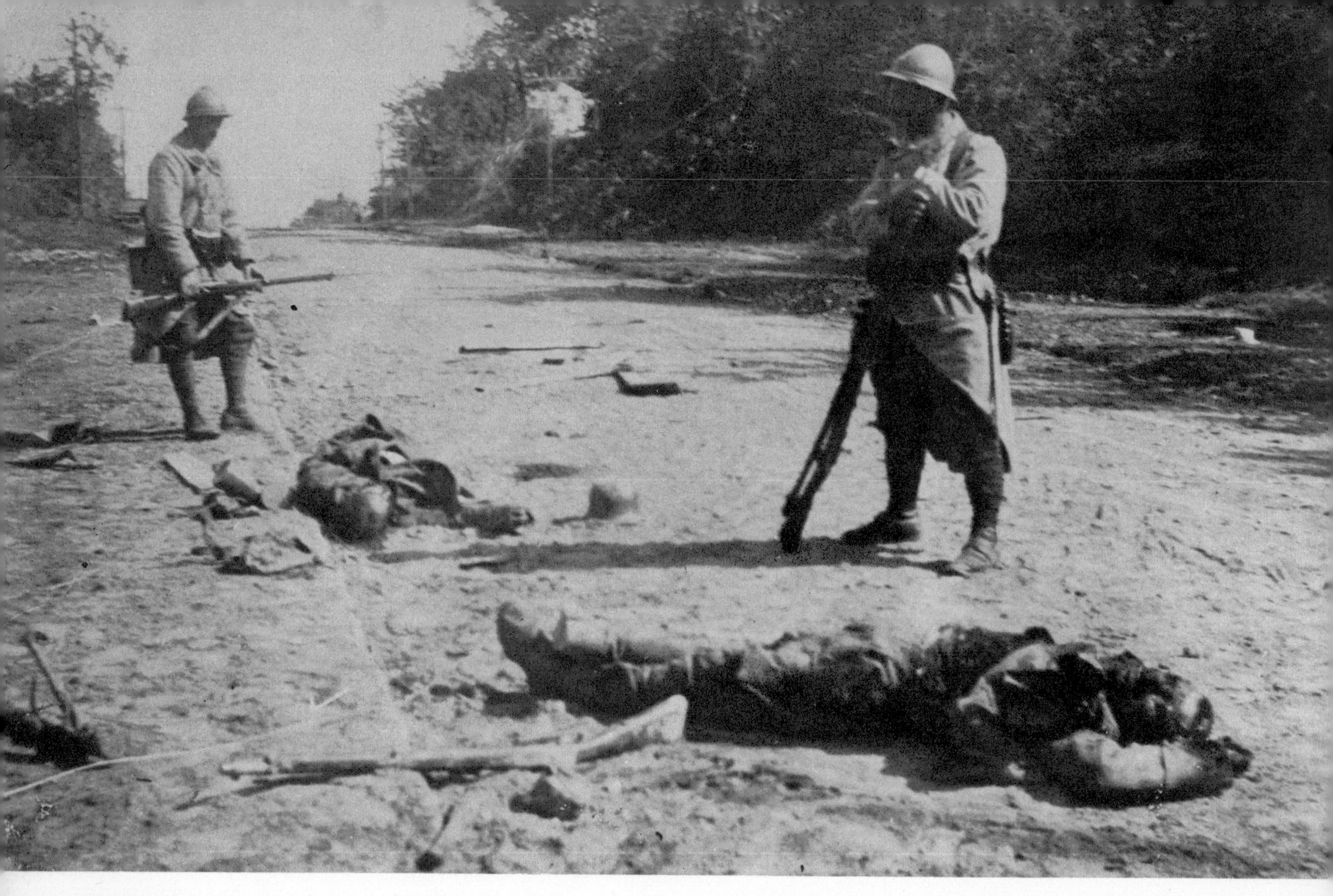

DETOUR

"All the News that's Fit to Print."

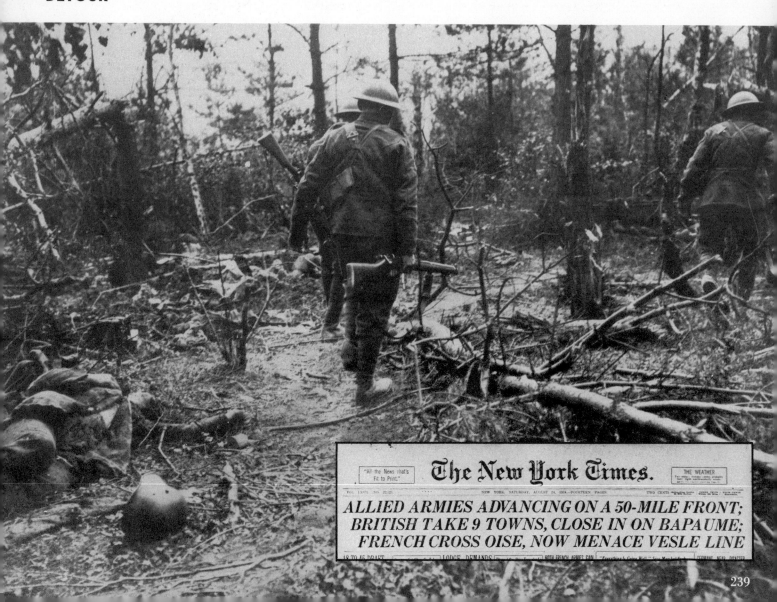

The New York Times.

THE WEATHER

VOL. LXVII. NO. 22,125. NEW YORK, SATURDAY, AUGUST 24, 1918.—FOURTEEN PAGES. TWO CENTS

ALLIED ARMIES ADVANCING ON A 50-MILE FRONT; BRITISH TAKE 9 TOWNS, CLOSE IN ON BAPAUME; FRENCH CROSS OISE, NOW MENACE VESLE LINE

18 TO 46 DRAFT — LODGE DEMANDS — BOTH FRENCH ARMIES GAIN — "Everything Is Going Well," Says Marshal Foch — GERMANS NEAR DISASTER

THE BIG PARADE

LISTENING POST

"All the News That's Fit to Print."

The New York Times.

THE WEATHER

NEW YORK, FRIDAY, AUGUST 2, 1918.—TWENTY PAGES. TWO CENTS

ENEMY RETREATS AFTER NEW ALLIED DRIVE; MANY PRISONERS TAKEN, TOTAL NOW 33,400; FOE FIGHTS ON AT OWN COST---LLOYD GEORGE

OPEN NEW SUBWAY LINES TO TRAFFIC;

U-Boat Menace No Longer a Real Factor, Says Daniels

PUNISHMENT FOR GERMANY

Longer War Lasts Sterner

Allies' Fresh Reserves Now Outnumber Foe's

AMERICANS AGAIN ADVANCE

German Shock Troops

Official Reports on New Allied Attack

French

German

STROKE ON 10-MILE FRONT

Towns and Heights Won

TRANSPORT

MINE SWEEPER

SURRENDER

WHIPPETS

GRENADES

END OF THE ROMANOFFS

CROWN JEWELS

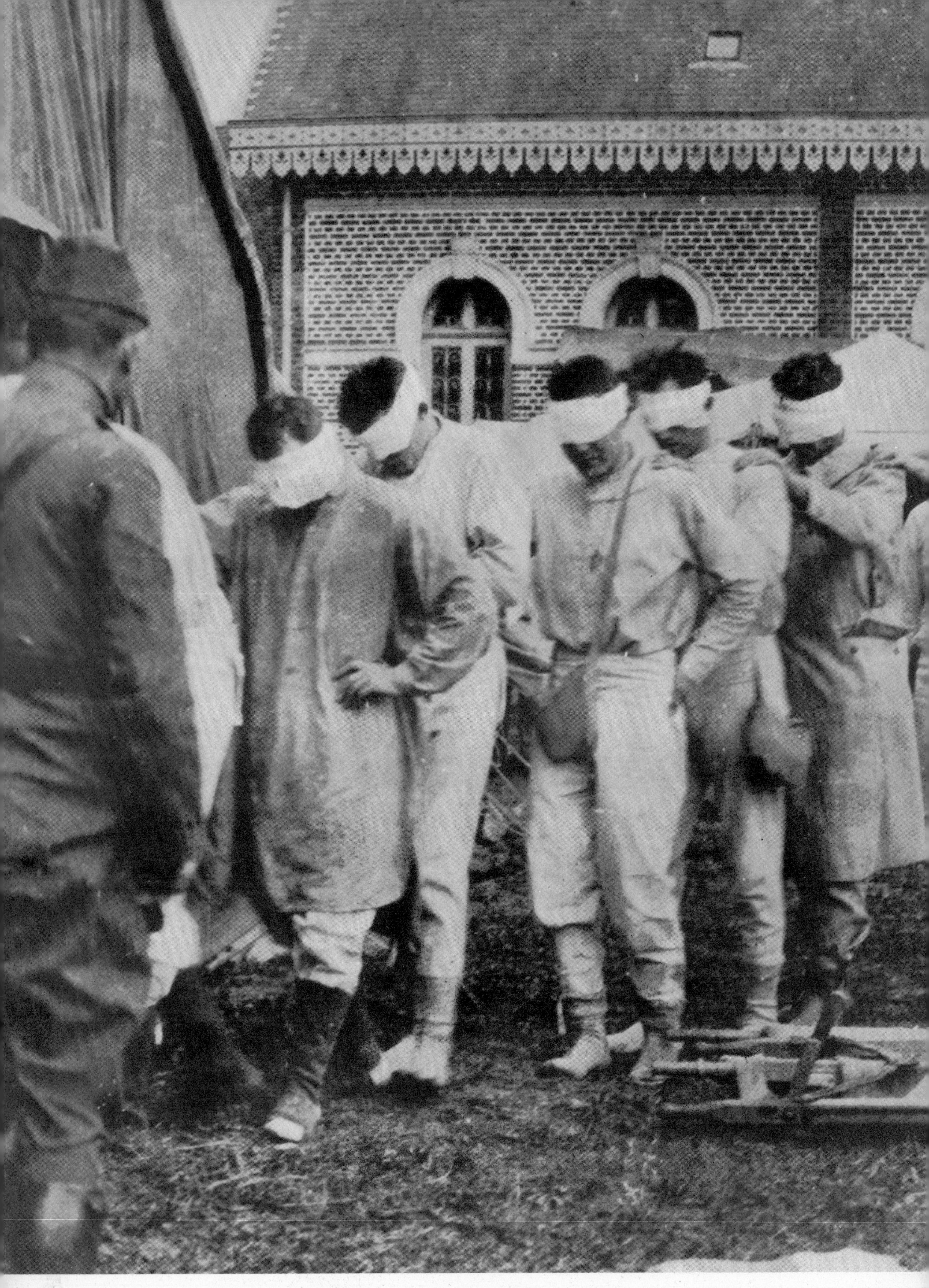

TWILIGHT

LINE OF DUTY

GAS ALARM

ARGONNE FOREST

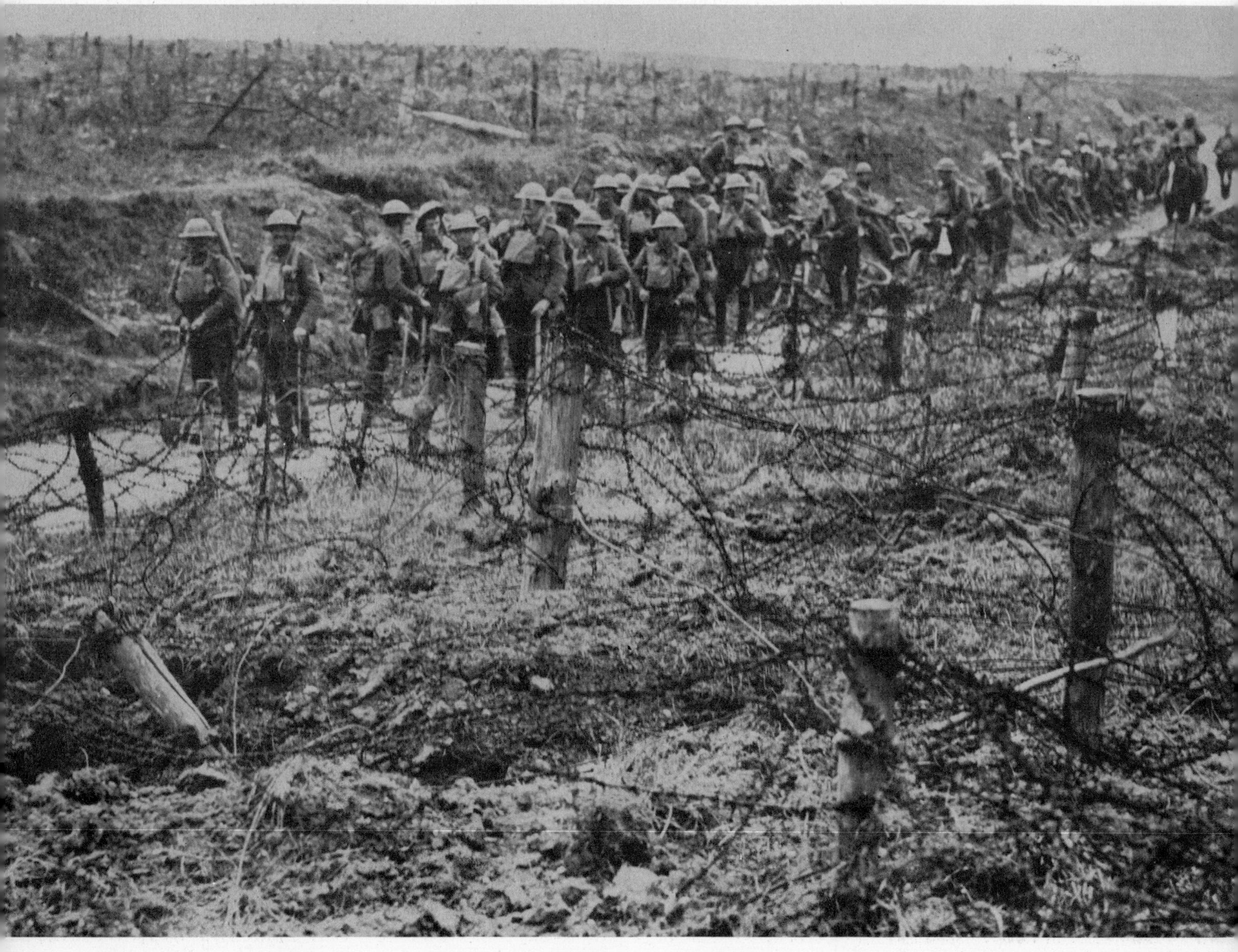

CLEAR ALL WIRES

"A-HUNTING WE WILL GO . . ."

Never say die!

Don't die till you have to!

What business have you to die for France, for Alsace-Lorraine, or for England in France?

Isn't it better anyhow to live than to die, no matter for how "glorious" a cause? Isn't it better to live and come back to the old folks at home, than to rot in the shell holes and trenches of France?

You have had to hear many high falutin words about "liberty", "humanity" and "making the world safe for democracy" but honest now, aren't these catch words merely sugar coating to the bitter pill of making you spend [illegible] those German soldier boys in their faded grey uniforms on the other side of "No Man's Land" are hot on the trail of your liberties?

Just like you, they want the war to end with honor so they can go back to their home folks. All they want is a chance to live and let live.

And so, if it should happen to you to fall into their hands you will find that they will treat you fair enough on the principle of **"live and let live".** Why run any more chances than you have to, you might as well be a free boarder in Germany till the war is over. **You don't want to die till you have to!**

PROPAGANDA DROPPED FROM GERMAN PLANES OVER THE AMERICAN LINES

Offizielle Zahlen.

Die zwischen dem 1. und 30. September eingebrachte Kriegsbeute der Armeen der Entente auf der Westfront beträgt:

2.844 Offiziere
120.292 Mann
1.500 Geschütze
über **10.000** Maschinengewehre.

Die **Gesamtbeute,** die von den verbündeten Armeen auf **allen** Kriegsschauplätzen zwischen dem 15. Juli und 30. September eingebracht wurde, beträgt:

5.518 Offiziere
248.494 Mann
3.669 Geschütze
über **23.000** Mäschinengewehre.

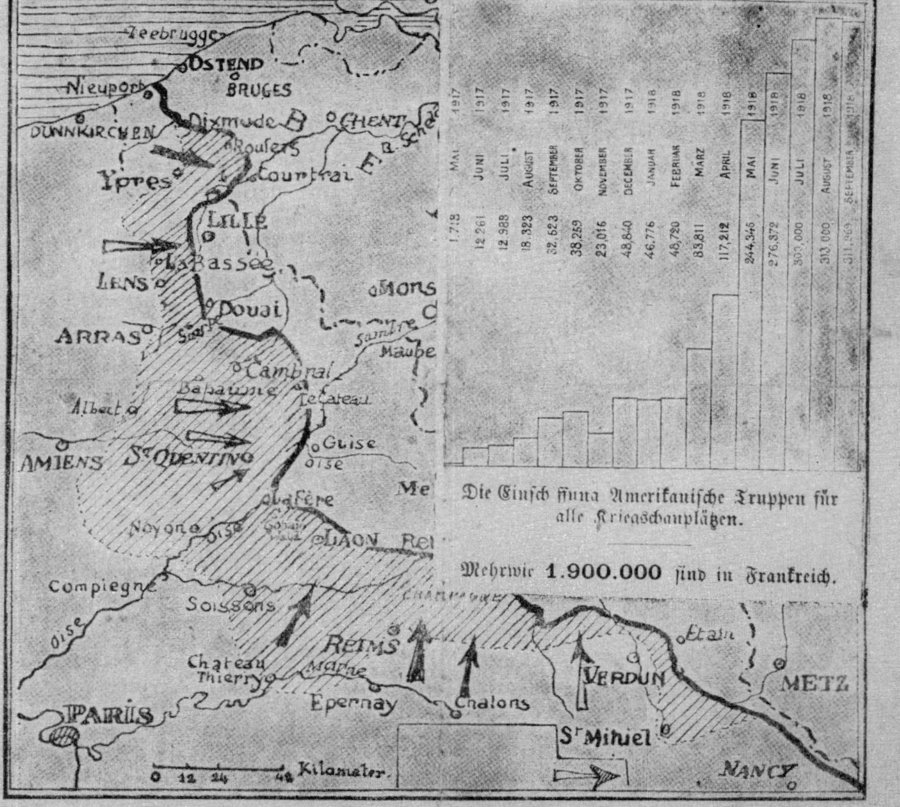

Der Deutsche Rückzug von 15 Juli an 10 Oktober 1918.

Einige Fragen an die Deutschen Soldaten.

1. Werdet Ihr jemals wieder so stark sein als im Juli 1918?
2. Werden Eure Gegner täglich stärker oder schwächer?
3. Haben Euch die grausamen Verluste die Ihr 1918 erlitten habt, den Siegfrieden gebracht, den Euch Eure Führer versprochen haben?
4. Habt Ihr noch leiseste Hoffnung auf einen Sieg?
5. Wollt Ihr Euer Leben lassen in einem hoffnungslosen Kampf?

PROPAGANDA DROPPED FROM AMERICAN PLANES OVER THE GERMAN LINES

WEATHER FORECAST.
Fair to-day; to-morrow partly cloudy; moderate northeast winds.

The Sun.

IT SHINES FOR ALL

VOL. LXXXVI.—NO. 11. NEW YORK, WEDNESDAY, SEPTEMBER 11, 1918. PRICE TWO CENTS.

HINDENBURG LINE PRACTICALLY WIPED OUT; FOCH IS CIRCLING ST. GOBAIN FOREST BASE; FRENCH AND BRITISH AT GATES OF ST. QUENTIN

McADOO DEMANDS TAX FREE LIBERTY BONDS WITH A $30,000 LIMIT

19-20 AND 32-36 FIRST CALLED IN NEW WAR DRAFT

Scores in German Jails for Doubting "Victory"

GERMANS PUSH LIBERALS FORTH IN PEACE MOVE

GERMAN TROOPS TOLD THEY MUST END RETREATS

Captured Order Warns That Practice of Giving Up

Americans Aiding in Flanking Movement Against Chemin des Dames.

FALL OF LA FERE SEEN

MAP DETAIL

"All the News That's Fit to Print."

The New York Times.

THE WEATHER

VOL. LXVIII. NO. 22,146 ... NEW YORK, WEDNESDAY, OCTOBER 2, 1918.—TWENTY-FOUR PAGES. TWO CENTS

FRENCH IN ST. QUENTIN; WHOLE LINE ADVANCED; WAR'S FIERCEST FIGHTING ON CAMBRAI FRONT; WHOLE GERMAN CABINET OUT; RIOTS IN BERLIN

WHOLE CITY ASTIR | AUSTRIA SEEKS TO QUIT WAR | AMERICANS PUSH AHEAD | Bitterest Fighting of War North of Cambrai | EXPLOSIONS IN ST. QUENTIN

FAÇADE

TIME OUT

ONE MAN DOWN

THE QUICK AND THE DEAD

SOIXANTE-QUINZE

STROLLERS

INTO THE BLUE

"All the News That's Fit to Print."

The New York Times.

THE WEATHER

NEW YORK, THURSDAY, OCTOBER 10, 1918. TWENTY-FOUR PAGES. TWO CENTS

HAIG TAKES CAMBRAI, SMASHES 20-MILE FRONT, ADVANCES 9 MILES, ROUTS 30 GERMAN DIVISIONS, AND HOTLY PURSUES THE DISORDERED ENEMY; AMERICANS BREAK THROUGH KRIEMHILDE LINE

CAMBRAI: CONTACT PATROL

THE TOWN HALL

"All the News That's Fit to Print."

The New York Times.

THE WEATHER

NEW YORK, TUESDAY, NOVEMBER 5, 1918. TWENTY-FOUR PAGES. TWO CENTS

ALLIES FIX TERMS THAT GERMANY MUST TAKE; AUSTRIA HAS MADE A COMPLETE SURRENDER; HER ARMY BROKEN, 300,000 MEN CAPTURED; BRITISH BREAKTHROUGH, TAKE 10,000 GERMANS

REPORTS POINT TO A DEMOCRATIC

Passes Bill to Let Women Sit in House of Commons

HAIG WINS ON 30-MILE LINE

His Troops Advancing

Wilson Congratulates The King of Italy

AUSTRIAN ARMY DESTROYED

300,000 Prisoners and

Allies Agree on Terms for Germany.

WASHINGTON, Nov. 4.—Secretary Lansing issued this statement at 9 o'clock tonight:

STATEMENT BY LANSING

He Announces Full Ac-

"MERCI"

RETURN OF THE NATIVE

"TEN THOUSAND DOLLARS FOR THE FOLKS BACK HOME"

TAPS

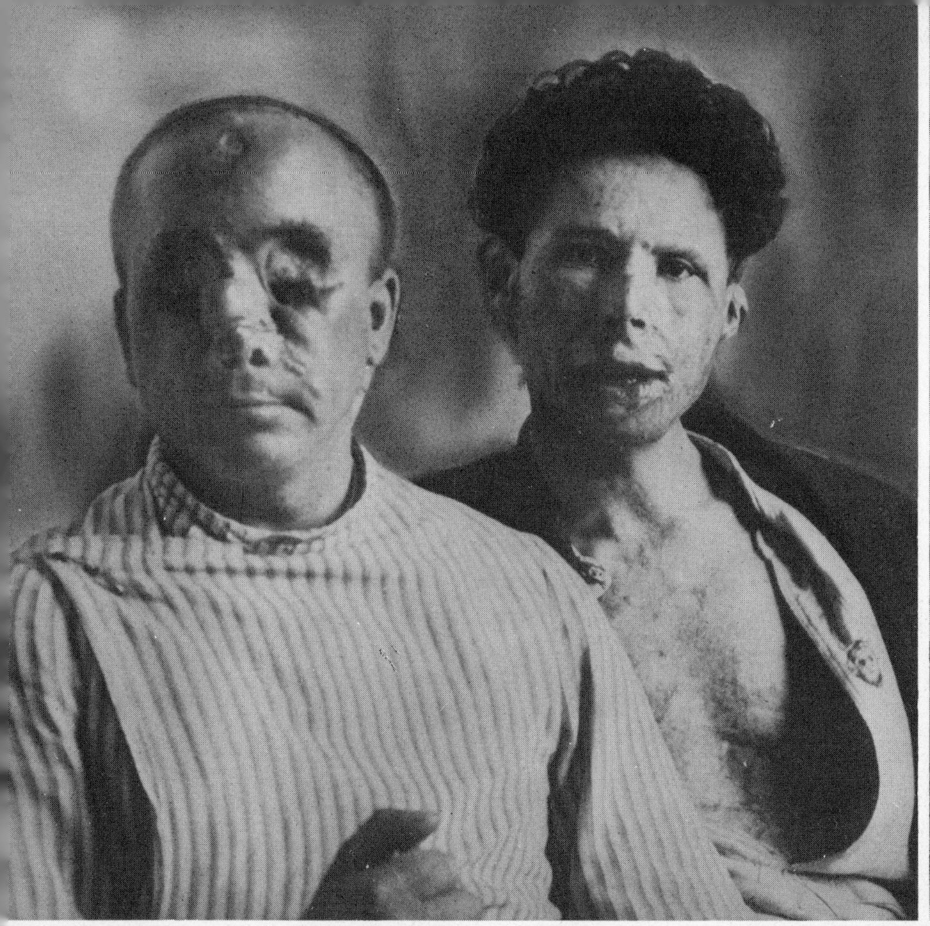

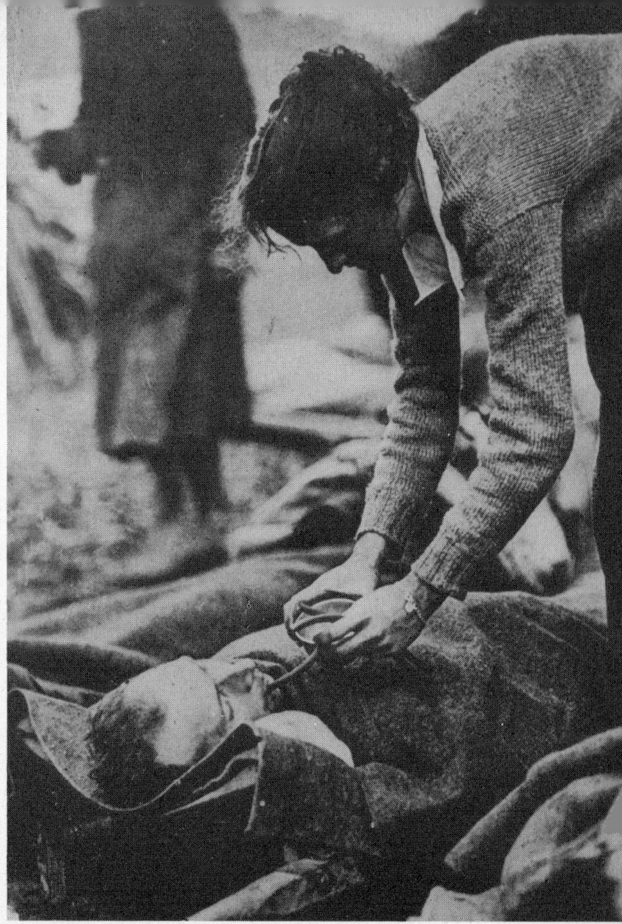

Ich verzichte hierdurch für alle Zukunft auf die Rechte an der Krone Preussen und die damit verbundenen Rechte an der deutschen Kaiserkrone.

Zugleich entbinde ich alle Beamten des Deutschen Reichs und Preussens sowie alle Offiziere, Unteroffiziere und Mannschaften der Marine, des Preussischen Heeres und der Truppen der Bundeskontingente des Treueides, des sie Mir als ihren Kaiser, König und Obersten Befehlshaber geleistet haben. Ich erwarte von ihnen, dass sie bis zur Neuordnung des Deutschen Reichs den Inhabern der tatsächlichen Gewalt in Deutschland helfen, das Deutsche Volk gegen die drohenden Gefahren der Anarchie, der Hungersnot und der Fremdherrschaft zu schützen.

Urkundlich unter Unserer Höchsteigenhändigen Unterschrift und beigedruckten Kaiserlichen Insiegel.

Gegeben Amerongen, den 28. November 1918.

Section 1 | "All the News That's Fit to Print." | **The New York Times.** | THE WEATHER | 1

NEW YORK, SUNDAY, NOVEMBER 10, 1918 — FIVE CENTS

KAISER AND CROWN PRINCE ABDICATE; NATION TO CHOOSE NEW GOVERNMENT; MAX IS REGENT; ARMISTICE DELAYED

FRENCH CROSS | GERMAN WARSHIPS CLASH | Geddes Sure the German Fleet Was Ordered Out. | SOCIALIST AS CHANCELLOR | Text of Decree Announcing Kaiser's Abdication

HOUSE HUNTING IN HOLLAND

SUCCESSOR TO THE HOHENZOLLERNS

BERLIN: STREET SCENE

"All the News That's Fit to Print."

The New York Times.

THE WEATHER

VOL. LXVIII. NO. 22,290. NEW YORK, FRIDAY, NOVEMBER 8, 1918. TWENTY-FOUR PAGES. TWO CENTS

GERMAN DELEGATES ON THE WAY TO MEET FOCH; FIRING STOPS ON ONE FRONT TO LET THEM PASS; GERMAN NAVY REBELS; OUR MEN TAKE SEDAN; FALSE PEACE REPORT ROUSES ALL AMERICA

CUT THROUGH SEDAN LINE

REDS SEIZE GERMAN NAVY

CITY GOES WILD WITH JOY

Text of Messages Exchanged About Armistice;

ROAD INDICATED TO ENVOYS

AMERICANS KILLED NOVEMBER 11TH

"All the News That's Fit to Print."

The New York Times.

THE WEATHER

VOL. LXVIII...NO. 22,206. NEW YORK, MONDAY, NOVEMBER 11, 1918. TWENTY-FOUR PAGES. TWO CENTS

ARMISTICE SIGNED, END OF THE WAR! BERLIN SEIZED BY REVOLUTIONISTS; NEW CHANCELLOR BEGS FOR ORDER; OUSTED KAISER FLEES TO HOLLAND

SON FLEES WITH EX-KAISER

Kaiser Fought Hindenburg's Call for Abdication;

BERLIN TROOPS JOIN REVOLT

Socialist Chancellor Appeals to All Germans

WAR ENDS AT 6 O'CLOCK THIS MORNING

CEASE FIRING!

FINAL NEWS EDITION

NEW YORK JOURNAL

FINAL NEWS EDITION

THURSDAY, NOVEMBER 7, 1918. TWO CENTS

GERMANY GIVES UP; WAR ENDS AT 2 P.M.

SMITH WINS BY 19,000 IN LATEST COUNT

VIEW OF KIEL AND HARBOR

HOSTILITIES CEASE; TRUCE IS SIGNED AT 11 A. M.

LONDON, Nov. 7.—Germany has accepted the armistice terms laid down by the

NEW YORK

PARIS

LONDON

THE AMERICANS MARCH INTO GERMANY

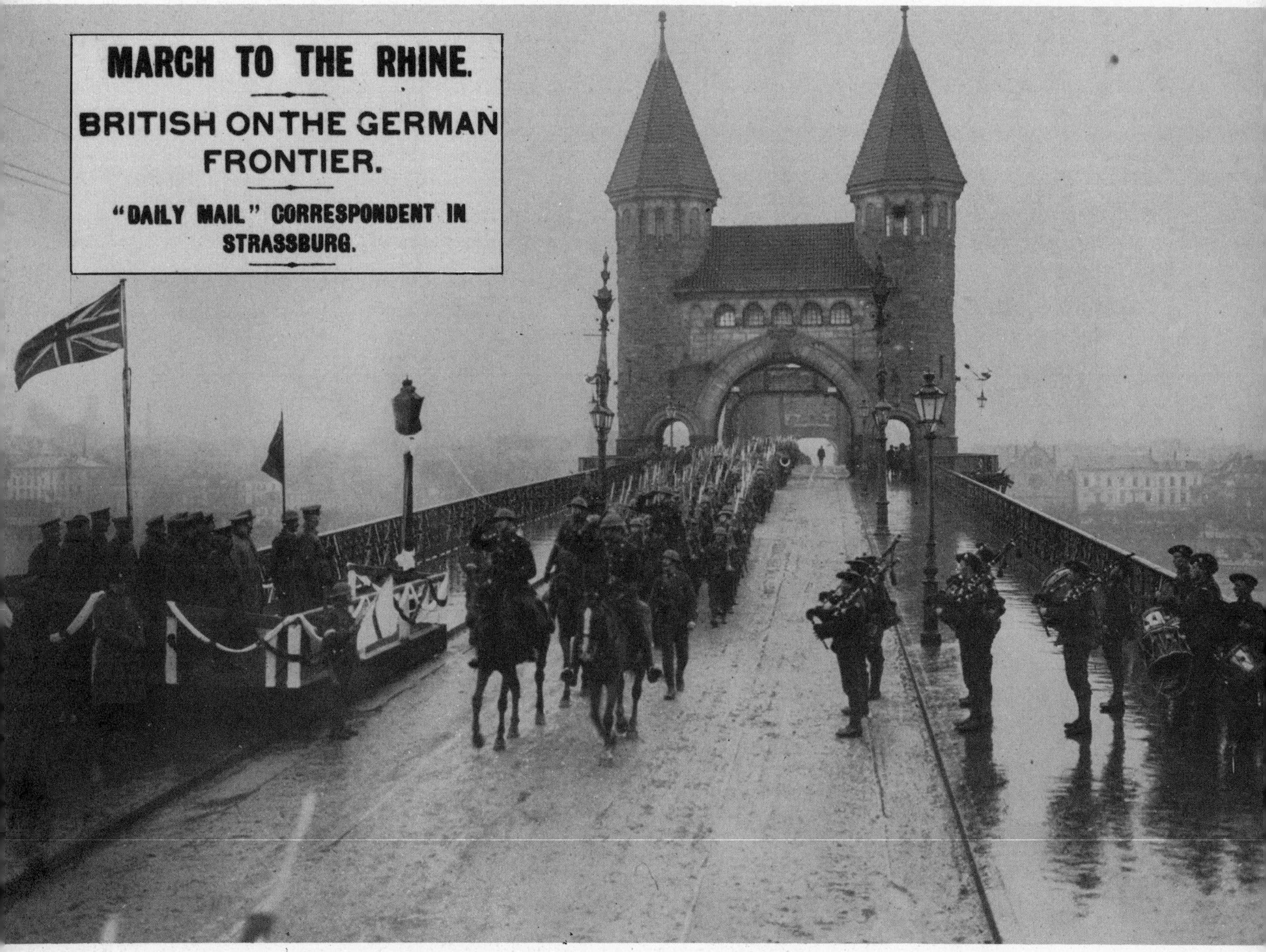

MARCH TO THE RHINE.

BRITISH ON THE GERMAN FRONTIER.

"DAILY MAIL" CORRESPONDENT IN STRASSBURG.

THE CANADIANS CROSS AT BONN

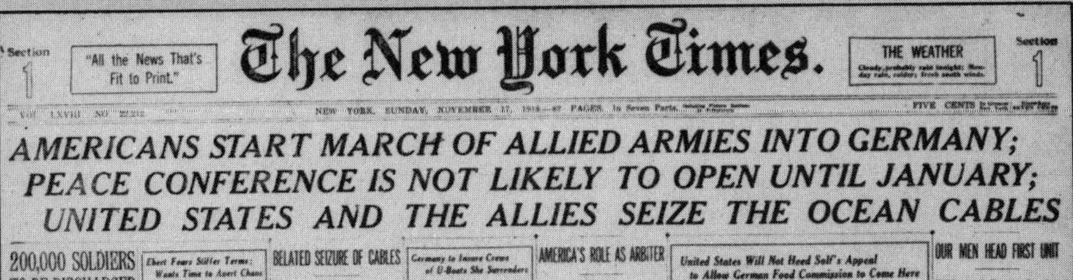

Section 1

"All the News That's Fit to Print."

The New York Times.

THE WEATHER

Section 1

NEW YORK, SUNDAY, NOVEMBER 17, 1918 — PAGES. In Seven Parts. FIVE CENTS

AMERICANS START MARCH OF ALLIED ARMIES INTO GERMANY; PEACE CONFERENCE IS NOT LIKELY TO OPEN UNTIL JANUARY; UNITED STATES AND THE ALLIES SEIZE THE OCEAN CABLES

200,000 SOLDIERS TO BE DISCHARGED

Ebert Fears Stiffer Terms; Wants Time to Avert Chaos

BELATED SEIZURE OF CABLES

Germany to Insure Crews of U-Boats She Surrenders

AMERICA'S ROLE AS ARBITER

United States Will Not Heed Solf's Appeal to Allow German Food Commission to Come Here

OUR MEN HEAD FIRST UNIT

Fifth and Tenth Armies

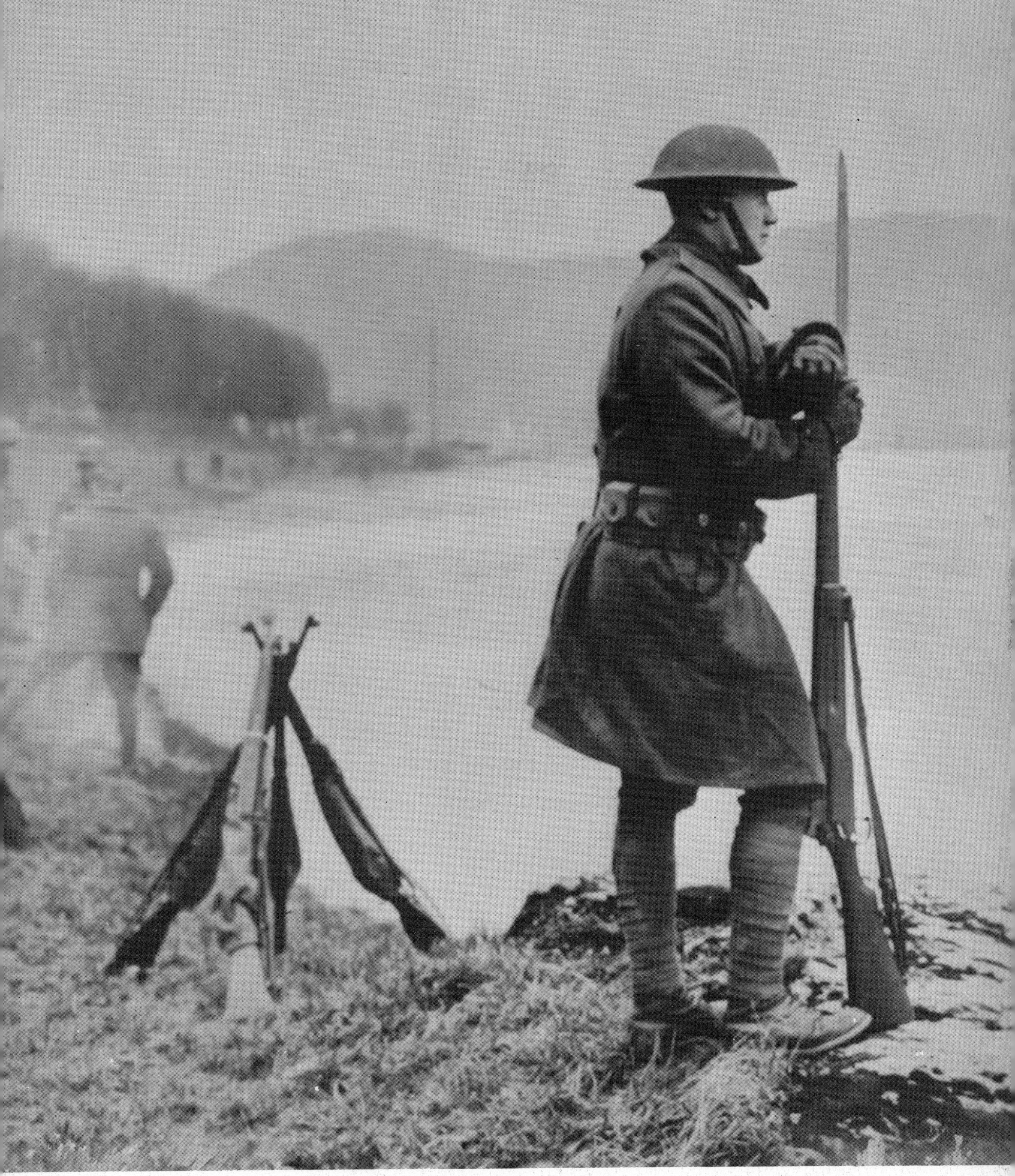

DIE WACHT AM RHEIN

JUNK

SCRAP

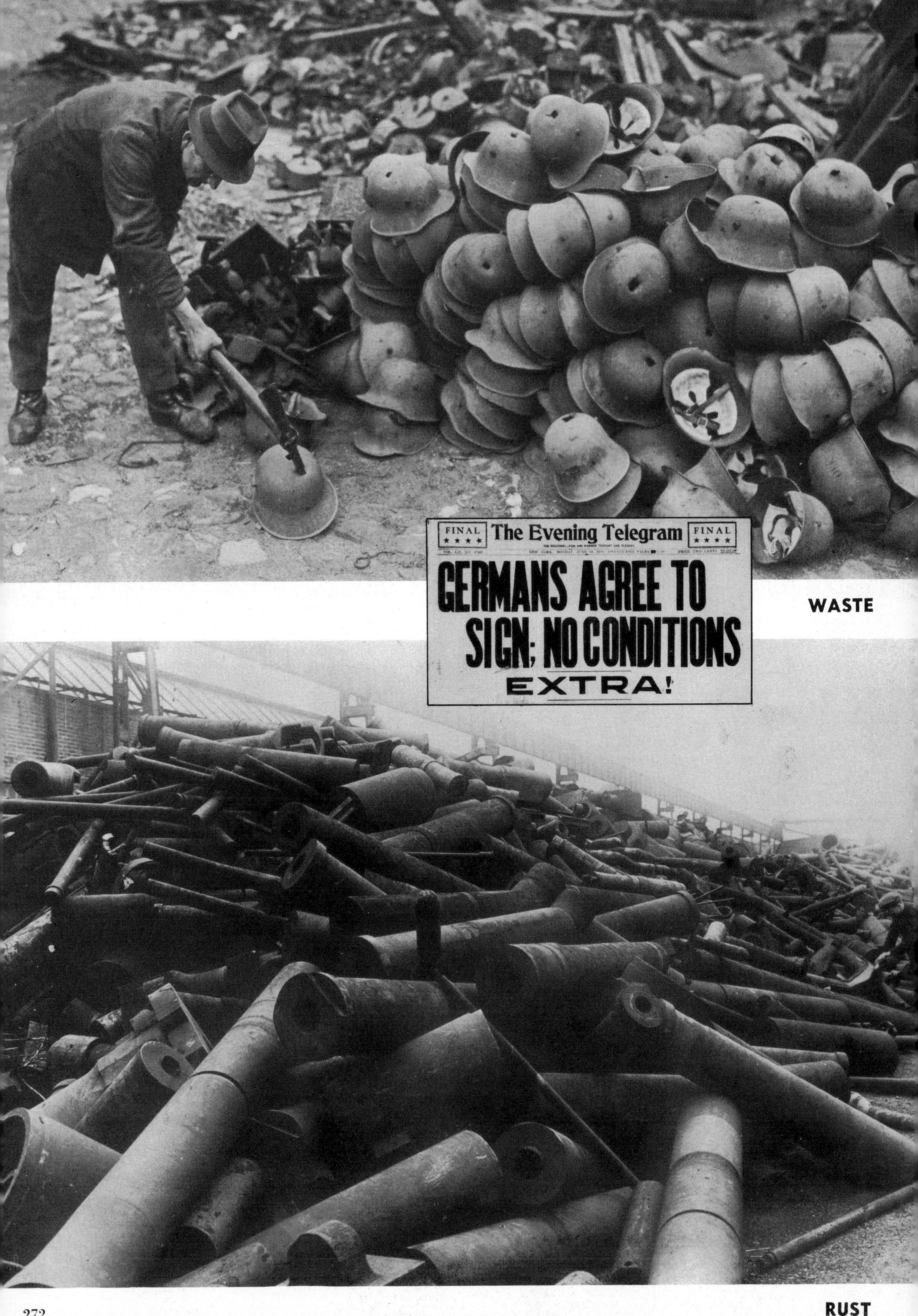
FINAL ★★★★
The Evening Telegram
FINAL ★★★★
GERMANS AGREE TO SIGN; NO CONDITIONS
EXTRA!

WASTE

RUST

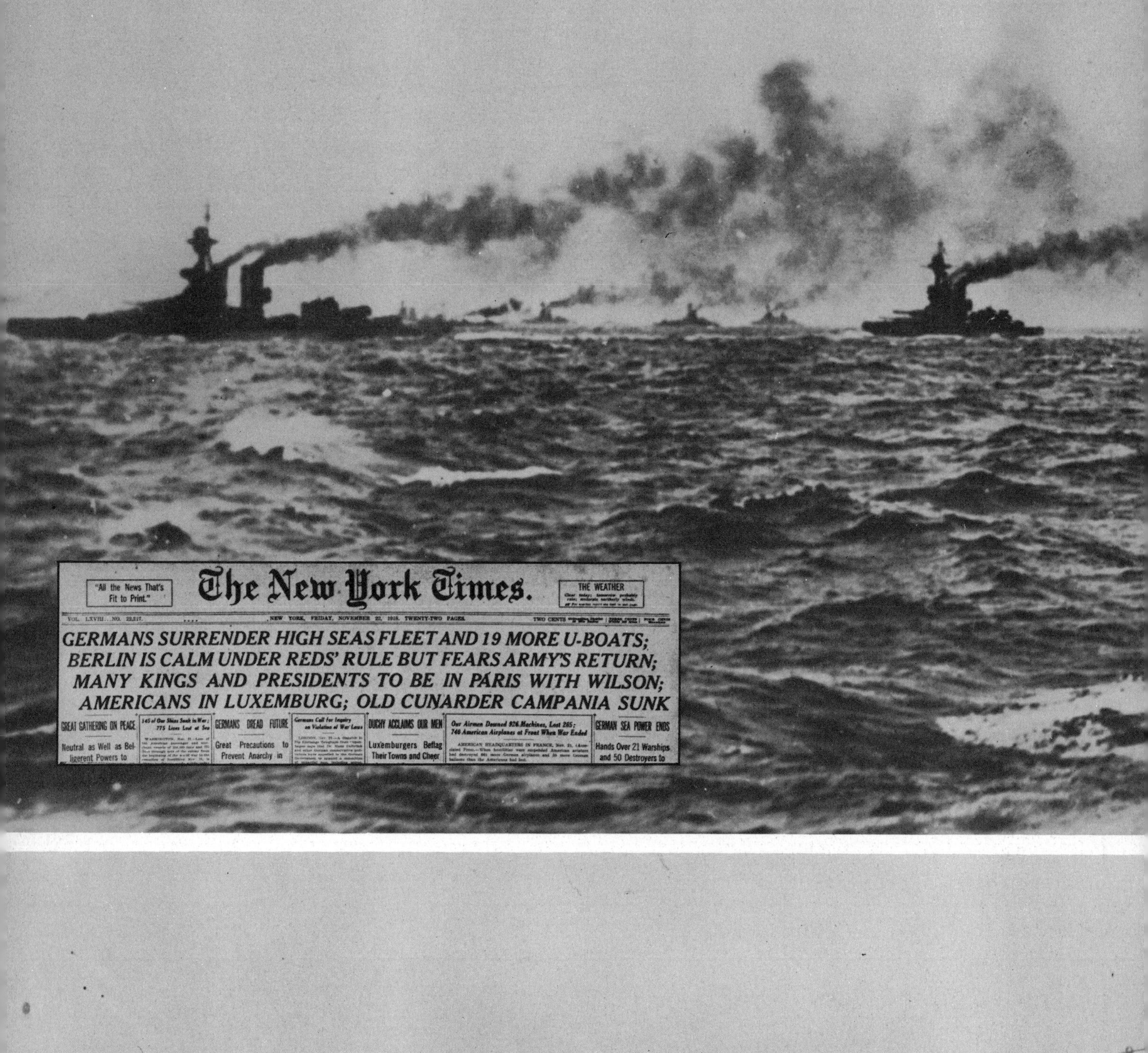

"All the News That's Fit to Print."

The New York Times.

THE WEATHER

VOL. LXVIII...NO. 22,217. NEW YORK, FRIDAY, NOVEMBER 22, 1918. TWENTY-TWO PAGES. TWO CENTS

GERMANS SURRENDER HIGH SEAS FLEET AND 19 MORE U-BOATS; BERLIN IS CALM UNDER REDS' RULE BUT FEARS ARMY'S RETURN; MANY KINGS AND PRESIDENTS TO BE IN PARIS WITH WILSON; AMERICANS IN LUXEMBURG; OLD CUNARDER CAMPANIA SUNK

GREAT GATHERING ON PEACE

Neutral as Well as Belligerent Powers to

145 of Our Ships Sunk in War; 775 Lives Lost at Sea

GERMANS DREAD FUTURE

Great Precautions to Prevent Anarchy in

Germans Call for Inquiry on Violation of War Laws

DUCHY ACCLAIMS OUR MEN

Luxemburgers Beflag Their Towns and Cheer

Our Airmen Downed 926 Machines, Lost 265; 740 American Airplanes at Front When War Ended

AMERICAN HEADQUARTERS IN FRANCE, Nov. 21.

GERMAN SEA POWER ENDS

Hands Over 21 Warships and 50 Destroyers to

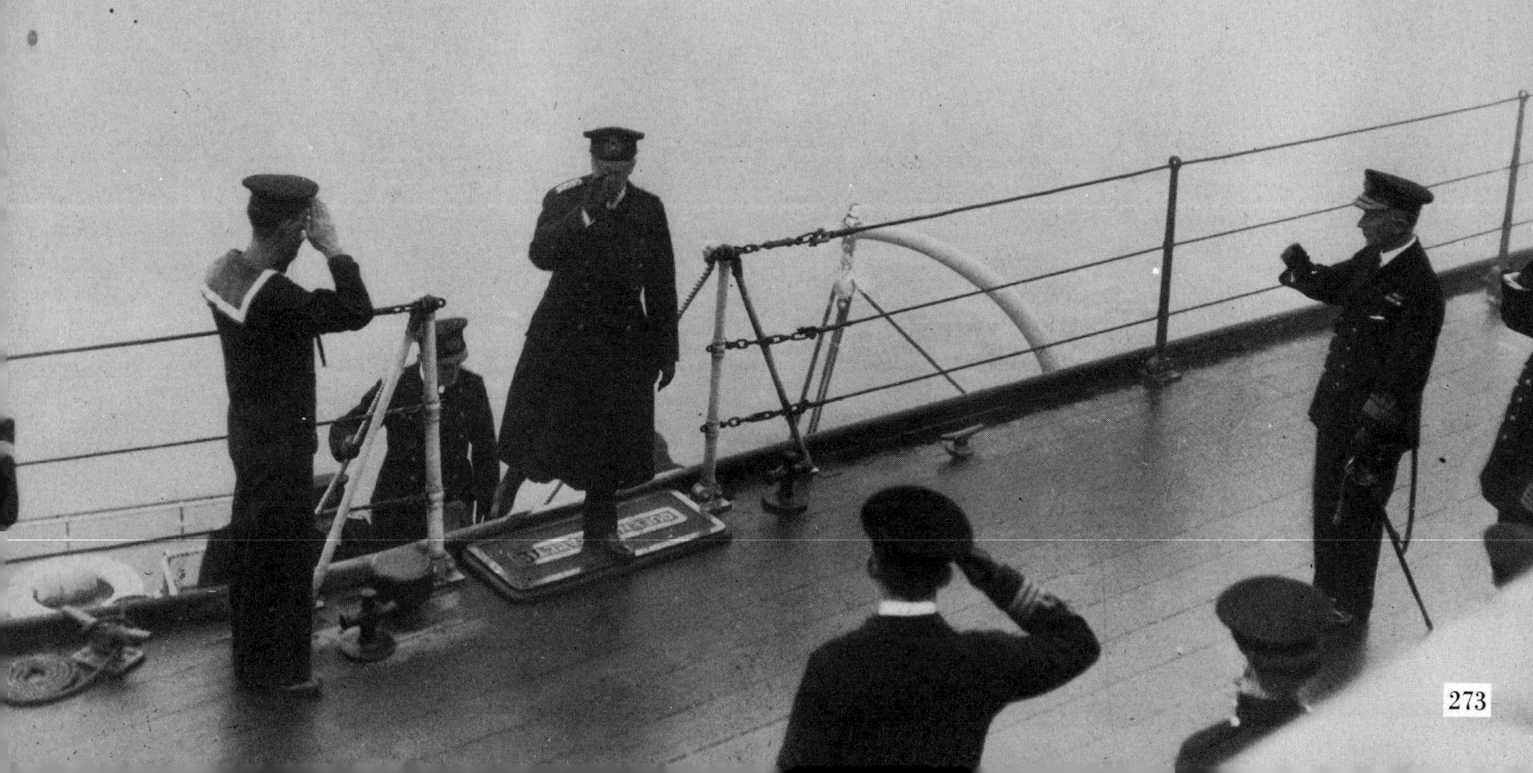

"BROTHERS, DON'T SHOOT!"

MUTINY — BERLIN

Vorwärts Buchdruckerei
anstalt Paul Singer
Gesells

END OF EXILE

". . . ÇA VA . . ."

". . . UPON THE NEXT GENERATION . . ."

"BUT THE VILLAGE IS NO LONGER THERE, MADAM"

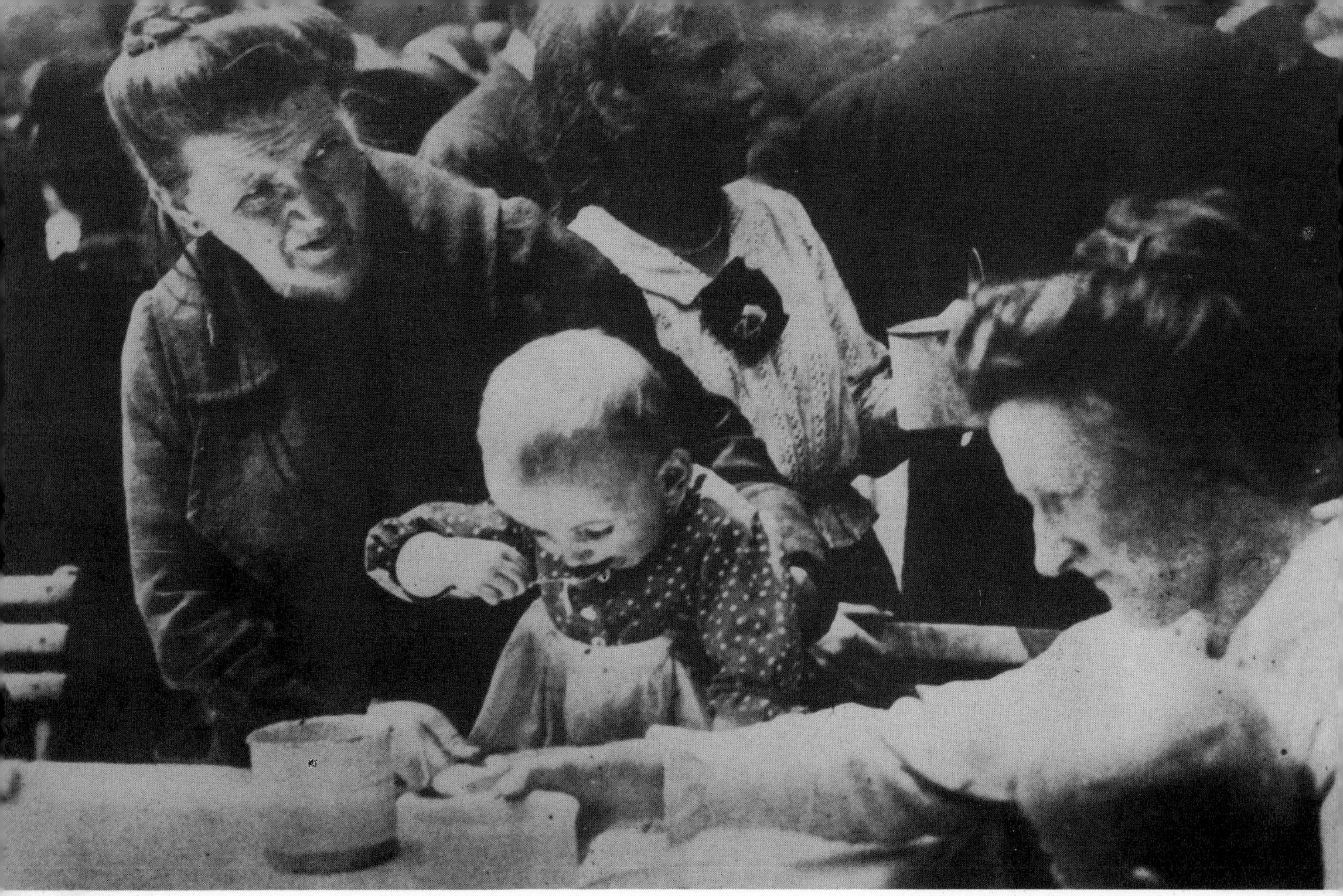

HUNGER

COLD

FAMINE

THE GLEANERS

CRUMBS

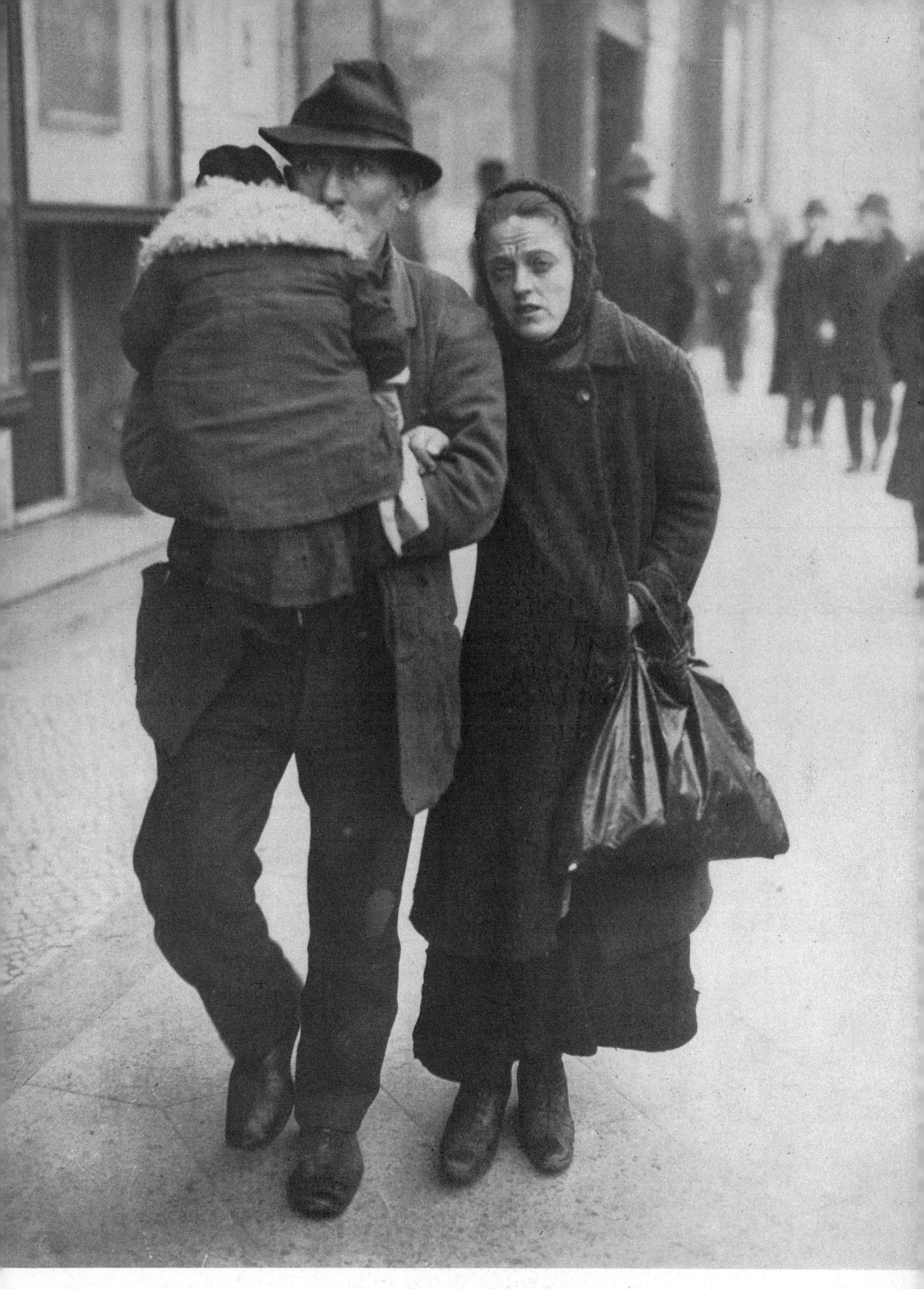

LITTLE MAN, WHAT NOW?

WHITE VICTIMS OF THE RED ARMY

RED VICTIMS OF THE WHITE ARMY

MORTS

KNOWN

UNKNOWN

Our Nation's Roll of Honor

Private John Paul Fedek
Detroit, Mich.,
Died of Wounds.

Private A. R. Minervini,
New York City,
Killed in Action.

Lieut. Lester Wallace Kearn
New York City,
Killed in Action.

Private Emile Blunschi,
Bernstadt, Ky.,
Killed in Action.

Lt. William C. Stevenson,
Mt. Pleasant, Penn.,
Killed in Action.

Sgt. Major Henry G. Bruce,
Minneapolis, Minn.,
Killed in Action.

Corp. George E. Brenner,
Syracuse, N. Y.,
Killed in Action.

Sergt. William J. Francis,
Brooklyn, N. Y.,
Killed in Action.

Corp. Christopher Doughty,
Fair Haven, N. J.,
Killed in Action.

Sergt. Gerold E. Dieterlen,
New York City,
Killed in Action.

Captain Otis H. King,
Hudson, Wis.,
Killed in Action.

Lieut. Hyman Freiberg,
New York City,
Killed in Action.

Private George Bauer,
Keokuk, Iowa,
Killed in Action.

Capt. Merritt Udell Lamb,
Rockford, Mich.,
Killed in Action.

Pvt. Edward C. Steckbauer,
Oshkosh, Wis.,
Killed in Action.

Capt. Charles A. Learned,
Detroit, Mich.,
Killed in Action.

Capt. Lee C. Lewis,
Olympia, Wash.,
Died of Wounds.

Sergt. Louis F. Antozak,
Detroit, Mich.
Killed in Action.

Capt. Joseph McConnell,
Killed in Action.
Phot by Bachrach, Boston.

Sergt. Walter Behler,
Hamburg, Penn.,
Killed in Action.

Sergt. George E. Mitchell,
Lents, Oregon,
Killed in Action.

...eorge Quincy Rice,
..., Mich.,
... Wounds.

Capt. Harol...
Ipav...
Killed in ...

...R. Watson,

Sergt. Edward F...
Brooklyn, N...
Killed in A...

...r William J.
Kansas City, ...
Killed in A...

THE CAPTAINS AND THE KINGS DEPART

THE ROLL OF HONOUR

THE FOLLOWING OFFICERS HAVE ALL DIED IN THE SERVICE OF THEIR COUNTRY, EITHER IN ACTION, FROM WOUNDS, OR OTHER CAUSES DIRECTLY INCIDENTAL TO THE GREAT WAR

Captain W. P. Stidston

Leinster Regt. He was the son of Mrs. and the late Rev. Stidston. He died of wounds

Captain G. J. Edwards

London Regiment (attd. King's Royal Rifles). He died of wounds received in action

Lieutenant W. T. C. Braine

West Riding Regiment. He had served through the campaign in German South-West Africa

Captain P. J. G. Ralph

Royal Irish Regt. He was twice mentioned in despatches and was killed in action

Captain A. L. Harris

Loyal North Lancs. Regt. He joined his regiment in August, 1914, and was killed on July 31

Lieutenant H. C. Pennington

Royal Fusiliers. He enlisted early in the war and was afterwards granted a commission

Lieutenant J. N. Taylor, M.C.

I.A.R.O. (attd. Indian Infantry). He died of wounds. Mentioned in despatches

Lieutenant R. L. Gammon

Australian Artillery. He was killed in action on August 1

2nd Lieutenant N. E. Baker

R.E. (attd. Tank Corps). He was the only surviving son of Mr. and Mrs. Ernest Baker

2nd Lieut. R. C. Chilvers

London Regiment. He joined the H.A.C. in 1914, afterwards obtaining a commission

Lieutenant C. E. A. Mahomed

Scots Guards. Only son of Mr. and Mrs. G. Mahomed. He returned from Argentina to serve

2nd Lieutenant B. W. White

R.F.C. He was the son of Mr. J. W. White, and was gazetted in 1916

2nd Lieutenant J. Miller, M.C.

Highland Light Infantry. Son of Mr. and Mrs. J. Miller. Awarded the Military Cross

Lieutenant C. F. Pittman

R.F.C. He had served in Egypt. Son of Mr. and Mrs. F. J. Pittman

2nd Lieut. M. Harvey-Jones, M.C.

Worcester Regt. (attd. Border Regt.). Son of Mr. and Mrs. A. Harvey Jones. He entered Sandhurst in 1914

The Rev. W. D. Geare

C.F. He was educated at Westminster and at Queen's College, Cambridge, and was gazetted chaplain to the forces in May, 1916. He was killed in action on July 31

Captain J. D. Venables-Llewellyn

Coldstream Guards. Son of Lieut.-Col. and Mrs. C. Venables-Llewellyn. He was educated at Eton and Sandhurst, and received his commission in January, 1915. He went to the front in October of that year

Captain W. N. Gourlay

Cameron Highlanders. He was educated first at Moorland House, Heswall, and afterwards at Radley College. Died from wounds

Captain C. Webster

R.F.A. He had travelled widely in the Pacific Islands and New Guinea, and was well known as an author and explorer. He was formerly in the Royal Artillery and joined up on the outbreak of war

Major A. J. Ross, D.S.O.

R.E. (attd. R.F.C.). He was educated at Malvern and Woolwich, obtaining his commission in 1900. He went to India in the following year. He served with the R.F.C. in Egypt and France

Pro patria mori

THE CAPTAINS AND THE KINGS DEPART

SUNRISE—1920

1933

1933

1933

1933

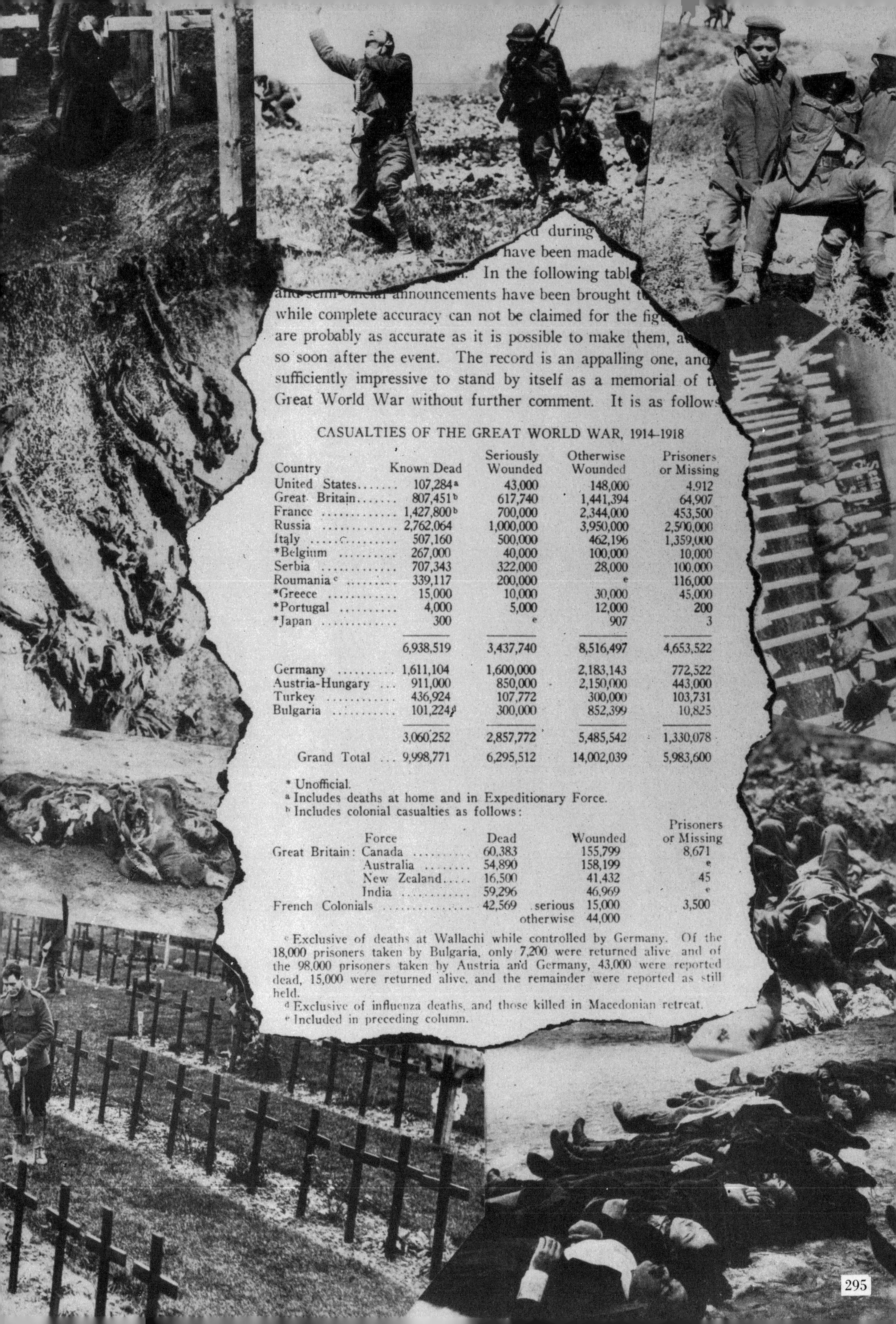

...d during ... have been made ... In the following tabl... and semi-official announcements have been brought t... while complete accuracy can not be claimed for the fig... are probably as accurate as it is possible to make them, a... so soon after the event. The record is an appalling one, and... sufficiently impressive to stand by itself as a memorial of t... Great World War without further comment. It is as follows

CASUALTIES OF THE GREAT WORLD WAR, 1914–1918

Country	Known Dead	Seriously Wounded	Otherwise Wounded	Prisoners or Missing
United States	107,284[a]	43,000	148,000	4,912
Great Britain	807,451[b]	617,740	1,441,394	64,907
France	1,427,800[b]	700,000	2,344,000	453,500
Russia	2,762,064	1,000,000	3,950,000	2,500,000
Italy	507,160	500,000	462,196	1,359,000
*Belgium	267,000	40,000	100,000	10,000
Serbia	707,343	322,000	28,000	100,000
Roumania[c]	339,117	200,000	e	116,000
*Greece	15,000	10,000	30,000	45,000
*Portugal	4,000	5,000	12,000	200
*Japan	300	e	907	3
	6,938,519	3,437,740	8,516,497	4,653,522
Germany	1,611,104	1,600,000	2,183,143	772,522
Austria-Hungary	911,000	850,000	2,150,000	443,000
Turkey	436,924	107,772	300,000	103,731
Bulgaria	101,224[d]	300,000	852,399	10,825
	3,060,252	2,857,772	5,485,542	1,330,078
Grand Total	9,998,771	6,295,512	14,002,039	5,983,600

* Unofficial.

[a] Includes deaths at home and in Expeditionary Force.

[b] Includes colonial casualties as follows:

	Force	Dead	Wounded	Prisoners or Missing
Great Britain:	Canada	60,383	155,799	8,671
	Australia	54,890	158,199	e
	New Zealand	16,500	41,432	45
	India	59,296	46,969	e
French Colonials		42,569	serious 15,000	3,500
			otherwise 44,000	

[c] Exclusive of deaths at Wallachi while controlled by Germany. Of the 18,000 prisoners taken by Bulgaria, only 7,200 were returned alive and of the 98,000 prisoners taken by Austria and Germany, 43,000 were reported dead, 15,000 were returned alive, and the remainder were reported as still held.

[d] Exclusive of influenza deaths, and those killed in Macedonian retreat.

[e] Included in preceding column.

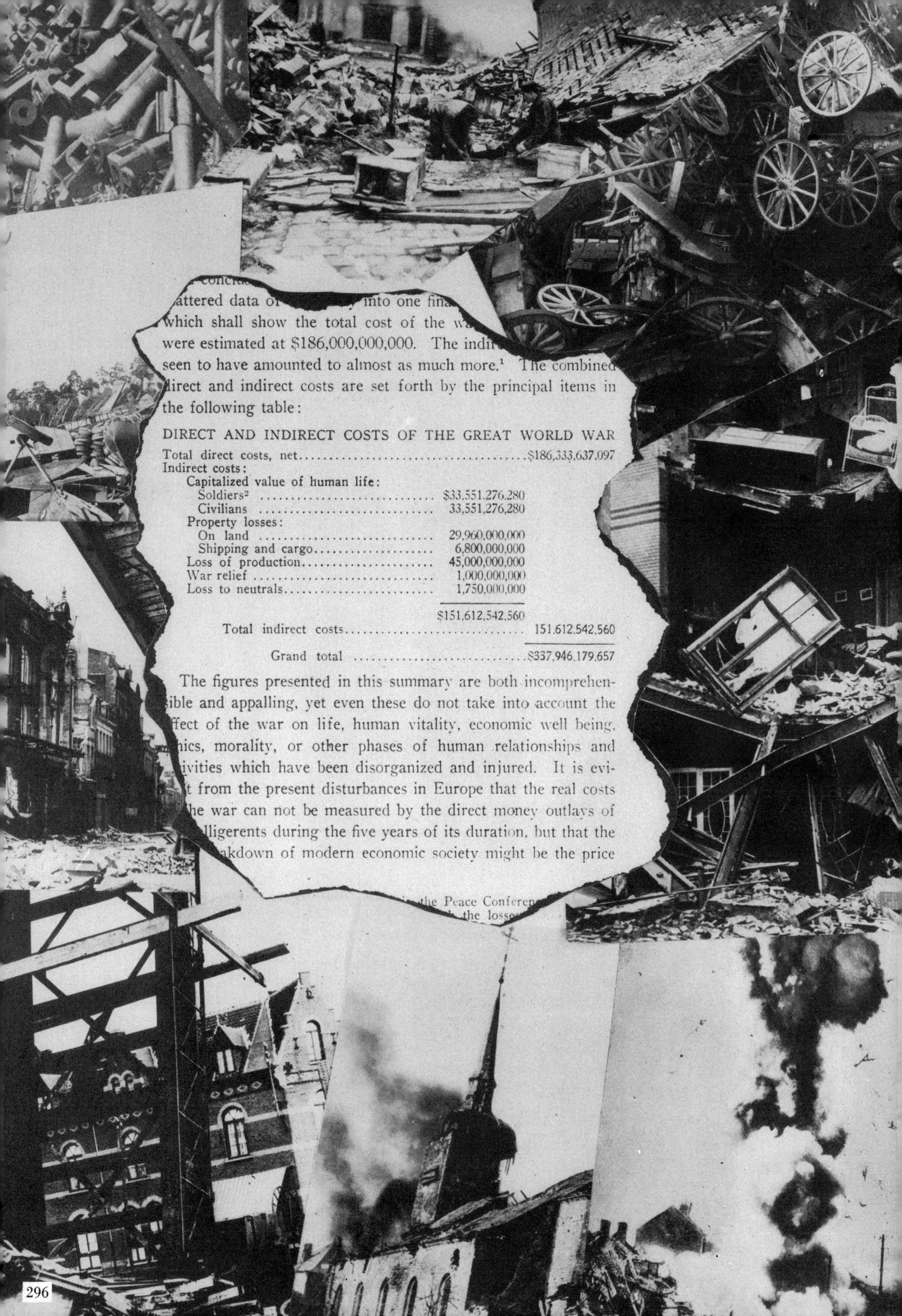

conclu

attered data of ... into one fina
which shall show the total cost of the wa
were estimated at $186,000,000,000. The indir
seen to have amounted to almost as much more.[1] The combined direct and indirect costs are set forth by the principal items in the following table:

DIRECT AND INDIRECT COSTS OF THE GREAT WORLD WAR

Total direct costs, net		$186,333,637,097
Indirect costs:		
Capitalized value of human life:		
Soldiers[2]	$33,551,276,280	
Civilians	33,551,276,280	
Property losses:		
On land	29,960,000,000	
Shipping and cargo	6,800,000,000	
Loss of production	45,000,000,000	
War relief	1,000,000,000	
Loss to neutrals	1,750,000,000	
	$151,612,542,560	
Total indirect costs		151,612,542,560
Grand total		$337,946,179,657

The figures presented in this summary are both incomprehen-sible and appalling, yet even these do not take into account the ffect of the war on life, human vitality, economic well being, hics, morality, or other phases of human relationships and ivities which have been disorganized and injured. It is evi-t from the present disturbances in Europe that the real costs he war can not be measured by the direct money outlays of lligerents during the five years of its duration, but that the akdown of modern economic society might be the price

the Peace Conferen
the losse

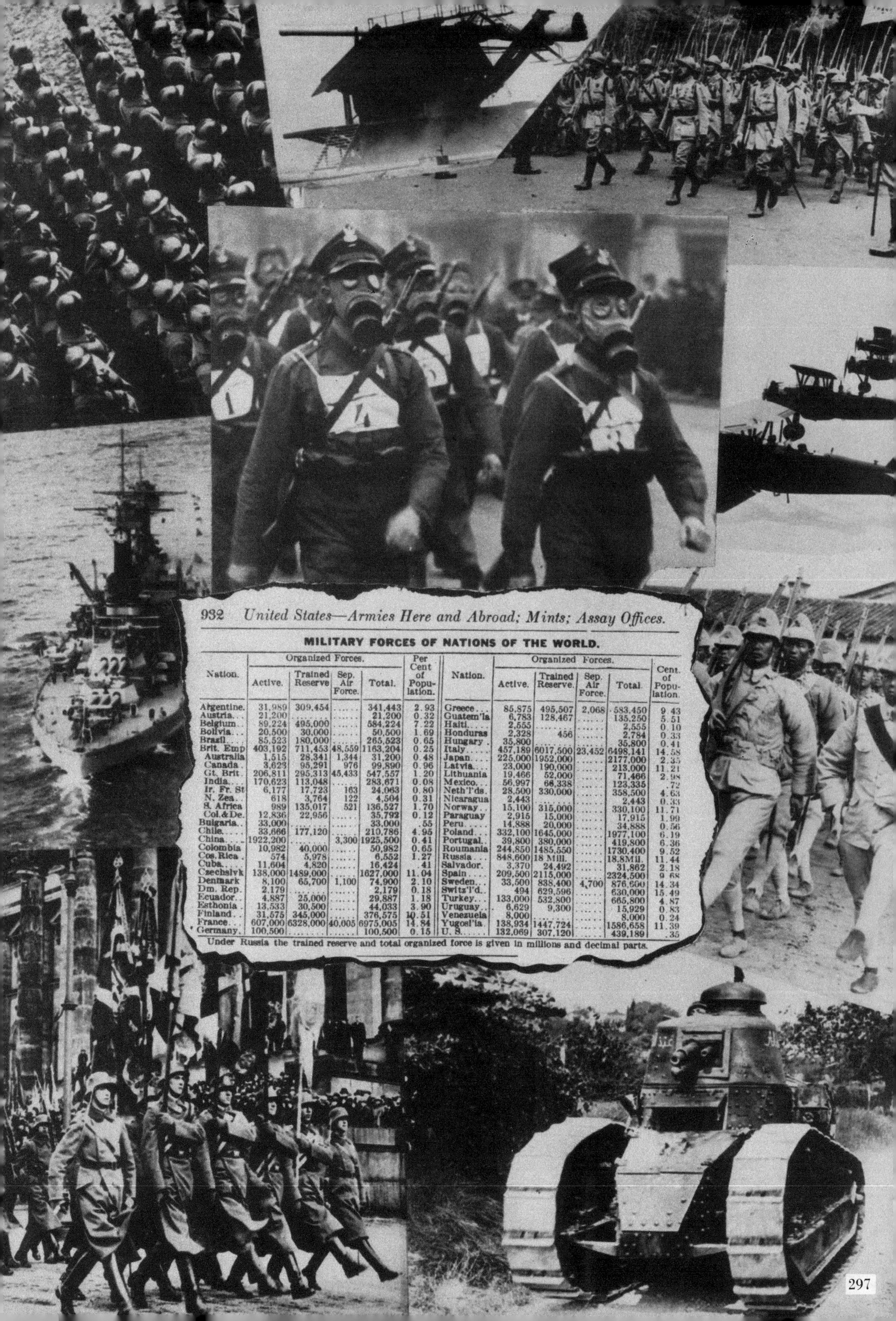

932 *United States—Armies Here and Abroad; Mints; Assay Offices.*

MILITARY FORCES OF NATIONS OF THE WORLD.

Nation.	Organized Forces. Active.	Trained Reserve	Sep. Air Force.	Total.	Per Cent of Population.	Nation.	Organized Forces. Active.	Trained Reserve.	Sep. Air Force.	Total.	Cent. of Population.
Argentine.	31,989	309,454	......	341,443	2.93	Greece...	85,875	495,507	2,068	583,450	9.43
Austria..	21,200	......	......	21,200	0.32	Guatem'la	6,783	128,467	......	135,250	5.51
Belgium..	89,224	495,000	......	584,224	7.22	Haiti....	2,555	......	......	2,555	0.10
Bolivia...	20,500	30,000	......	50,500	1.69	Honduras	2,328	456	......	2,784	0.33
Brazil...	85,523	180,000	......	265,523	0.65	Hungary.	35,800	......	......	35,800	0.41
Brit. Emp	403,192	711,453	48,559	1163,204	0.25	Italy.....	457,189	6017,500	23,452	6498,141	14.58
Australia	1,515	28,341	1,344	31,200	0.48	Japan....	225,000	1952,000	......	2177,000	2.35
Canada.	3,623	95,291	976	99,890	0.96	Latvia...	23,000	190,000	......	213,000	11.21
Gt. Brit.	206,811	295,313	45,433	547,557	1.20	Lithuania	19,466	52,000	......	71,466	2.98
India...	170,623	113,048	......	283,671	0.08	Mexico..	56,997	66,338	......	123,335	.72
Ir. Fr. St	6,177	17,723	163	24,063	0.80	Neth'l'ds.	28,500	330,000	......	358,500	4.63
N. Zea..	618	3,764	122	4,504	0.31	Nicaragua	2,443	......	......	2,443	0.33
S. Africa	989	135,017	521	136,527	1.70	Norway..	15,100	315,000	......	330,100	11.71
Col.&De.	12,836	22,956	......	35,792	0.12	Paraguay	2,915	15,000	......	17,915	1.99
Bulgaria..	33,000	......	......	33,000	.55	Peru.....	14,888	20,000	......	34,888	0.56
Chile....	33,666	177,120	......	210,786	4.95	Poland...	332,100	1645,000	......	1977,100	6.19
China...	1922,200	......	3,300	1925,500	0.41	Portugal..	39,800	380,000	......	419,800	6.36
Colombia	10,982	40,000	......	50,982	0.65	Roumania	244,850	1485,550	......	1730,400	9.52
Cos. Rica.	574	5,978	......	6,552	1.27	Russia...	848,600	18 Mill.	......	18.8Mil.	11.44
Cuba....	11,604	4,820	......	16,424	.41	Salvador.	3,370	24,492	......	31,862	2.18
Czechslvk	138,000	1489,000	......	1627,000	11.04	Spain....	209,500	2115,000	......	2324,500	9.68
Denmark	8,100	65,700	1,100	74,900	2.10	Sweden...	33,500	838,400	4,700	876,600	14.34
Dm. Rep.	2,179	......	......	2,179	0.18	Switz'l'd..	494	629,596	......	630,000	15.49
Ecuador..	4,887	25,000	......	29,887	1.18	Turkey...	133,000	532,800	......	665,800	4.87
Esthonia.	13,533	30,500	......	44,033	3.90	Uruguay..	6,629	9,300	......	15,929	0.83
Finland..	31,575	345,000	......	376,575	10.51	Venezuela	8,000	......	......	8,000	0.24
France...	607,000	6328,000	40,005	6975,005	14.84	Yugosl'ia.	138,934	1447,724	......	1586,658	11.39
Germany.	100,500	......	......	100,500	0.15	U. S.....	132,069	307,120	......	439,189	.35

Under Russia the trained reserve and total organized force is given in millions and decimal parts.

Complete Bid and Asked
New York Evening Post
BASEBALL FINAL
Complete Bid and Asked
THREE 3 CENTS
TUESDAY, MAY 16, 1933
ROOSEVELT WARNS WORLD TO END WAR, CUT ARMS; ARRAIGNS OBSTRUCTIONISTS
Score 2 on Cubs
MITCHELL DEAL CALLED THEFT
MESSAGE GIVES PLAN FOR PACT
Roosevelt Text
APPEAL WARNS 54 NATIONS TO AID PEACE AIMS
Paris Awaiting Debt Statement From America
Army of Vagabond Boys Gets Little Help in South
$1,000,000 SET ASIDE FOR JOB RELIEF HERE
Europe Swims In Fascist Tide, Mussolini Says
'That Which We Willed in '19 Reality Today in Italy,' Il Duce Tells Black Shirts
of Ideal Hailed
CALLS DEPRESSION WAR'S LAST BATTLE
Dr. Shotwell Reports to the Carnegie Endowment That Conflict Shattered Faith.
"A MORTGAGE ON FUTURE"
"Prosperity of Years to Come as Well as of Those Gone By" Is Destroyed, He Declares.
Dr. James T. Shotwell, Professor of History at Columbia University and director of the division of economics and history of the Carnegie Endowment for International
THE NEW YORK TIMES, MONDAY, APRIL 24, 1933.
U. S. PROPOSES ARMS CONTROL
GENEVA, April 26 (AP).—Prest
TO AID JOBLESS
Britain Studies Dual System to Supplant Dole
TOKIO TO EXTEND WAR OPERATIONS
Japan Wrecks League Efforts To Conciliate Far East Dispute
JAPANESE BUY $8,000,000 ARMS
NIGHT EDITION
The Sun
NIGHT EDITION With Wall Street Closing
NEW YORK, TUESDAY, MAY 16, 1933.
PRICE THREE CENTS.
ROOSEVELT SOUNDS WORLD PEACE CALL
Text of President's Message To the Heads of 54 Nations
PRESIDENT SAYS SELFISH ACTS IMPERIL PEACE
ASKS NATIONS TO DROP AGGRESSIVE WEAPONS
CONGRESSMAN
$500,000,000 Bill For Relief O. K.'d By Senate Body

NOTES ON THE PHOTOGRAPHS

(the numbers refer to pages)

PAGE	
1	*Top:* The Congress of Vienna, 1815, when the Principal Powers met to re-draw the map of Europe. *Center—Left:* Bismarck dictating the terms of peace to France at the conclusion of the Franco-German War, 1871. *Bottom:* The Algericas conference, 1906, where conflicting interests between Germany and France in Northern Africa were adjusted.
7	*Top:* Berlin, Unter Den Linden. *Bottom:* Buckingham Palace, London.
8	*Top:* Le Matin Office, Paris. *Bottom:* Main Square, Belgrade, Serbia.
12	*Top:* German Reservists parading on Broadway, New York City, August 4, 1914. *Center:* American tourists who had been caught in the War Zone return home on the U. S. Cruiser *Cincinnati.* *Bottom:* German Nationals in London rounded up for deportation.
13	Belgian refugees leaving their homes near the frontier, to escape the advancing German armies, August, 1914.
14	*Top:* Belgian infantry outposts with machine guns. *Bottom:* The first Germans enter Brussels.
15	German 21 cm. Howitzer type siege gun used in bombardment of the Belgian forts.
16	Ruins of a fortress in Antwerp.
20	The Belgian town of Malines after bombardment by the Germans.
21	*Top:* Belgian refugees en route from Ostend to England. *Center:* Belgian volunteers join the colors. *Bottom:* Belgians of military age taken as prisoners of War to Germany.
25	*Bottom:* Belgian children parading in honor of their Allies.
26	British women flaunting petticoats for men who do not volunteer.
27	*Bottom:* Part of "the first hundred thousand" drilling in streets, owing to shortage of barracks in England.

PAGE	
28	*Top:* The Mayor of a German garrison town addresses the parting soldiers. *Bottom:* Refugees from occupied French territory reading messages left on window shutters by those who had fled before them.
29–30	Russian infantry.
29	(*Insert*) Refugees from East Prussia.
31	German infantry with machine guns on fortified banks of the Vistula river.
35	*Top:* In Berlin.
36	*Top:* In Paris.
37	*Top:* French Artillery at the First Battle of the Marne, September, 1914. *Bottom:* German prisoners captured at the Marne.
38	"I had a fair Fatherland: it was a dream."
39–40	*Top:* French infantry fighting in the open at the Marne. (At this time the French troops still wore the time-honored red pants, dark blue coats, and caps.)
39	*Bottom:* General Gallieni, Military Governor of Paris, inspecting volunteers, as Germans get within striking distance.
43	Rheims Cathedral.
44	Façade of the Cathedral protected by sandbags.
46	*Top:* Women workers in French munitions factory. *Bottom:* Depositing war relief funds in dummy 42 cmm. shell in Vienna.
47–48	Torpedoed French Transport *Santay* sinking in the Mediterranean. (*Insert*) A German submarine.
49	King Peter of Serbia watching the retreat of his defeated army.
50	*Top:* Abandoned Austrian artillery in Serbia. *Bottom:* Exhausted Serbian soldiers at rest.
51	German prisoners of war in England.
52	French prisoners of war in Germany.

PAGE

258 *Top:* British entering Cambrai, October 9, 1918.
Bottom: Remains of the Town Hall, Cambrai.

259 French children cheering the victorious British at Lille, October 17, 1918.

260 *Top:* British troops in a liberated French village.
Bottom: French refugees return to find their homes in ruins.

261 *Top:* American casualties in the Argonne.

262 *Bottom:* American hospital in Paris.

263 The ex-Kaiser entering his home in Holland, November 10, 1918.

264 *Top:* President Ebert of the new Republic inspecting German troops.
Bottom: Revolution in Berlin.

265 *Top:* Graves of the last Americans killed near Sedan, November 11, 1918.
Bottom: The railroad car in which the Armistice was signed, November 11, 1918.

266 *Top:* American soldiers cheering the Armistice announcement, near Sedan, November 11, 1918.
Bottom: The last British shot is being officially photographed.

270 An American sentry on the Rhine, near Coblenz.

271–72 German War material destroyed under the terms of the Armistice.

273–74 *Top:* German fleet steaming toward the British Grand fleet for surrender, November 21, 1918.

273 *Bottom:* Admiral Von Meurer boards the British Flagship to report the surrender of the German fleet.

274 *Bottom:* A German U-Boat surrenders.

275 Revolution in Berlin.

276 Destruction of the Socialist paper *Vorwarts,* Berlin.

277 *Top:* Returning French refugees.
Bottom: Business as usual amidst the ruins.

278 *Top:* German orphans.
Bottom: Homeless refugees aided by Red Cross workers in Paris.

PAGE

279 *Top:* American food-relief station in Vienna.
Bottom: Red Cross supplies for war victims in Italy.

280 Result of post-war famine in Russia.

281 *Top:* German townspeople waiting to scour fields for potatoes left by the farmers.
Bottom: The poor of Berlin rummaging in refuse heaps.

283–84 Casualties of the Red and White Armies in Siberia.

285–86 The Allied troops parade through the Arc de Triomphe in Paris.

287–88 *Top:* One of the American cemeteries in France.

287 *Bottom:* Marshal Foch salutes the British Unknown Soldier.

288 *Bottom:* Bronze casket containing the Italian Unknown Soldier.

289–90 *Center Layout:* Reproduction of typical pages that appeared regularly in British and American periodicals, showing portraits of soldiers killed in action.

289 *Left Top:* Field Marshal Haig (England).
Left Center: Field Marshal Hindenburg (German).
Left Bottom: (left to right) General Gillain (Belgium), General Diaz (Italy), Marshal Foch (France), General Pershing (U. S.), Admiral Beatty (England).

290 *Right Top:* King Albert of Belgium.
Right Center: Marshal Joffre (France).
Bottom: Delegates to First International Disarmament Conference in Geneva.

291–92 Three men and one woman, convicted of treason during the War, are executed at Vincennes near Paris, 1920.

293 *Top:* Hitler.
Bottom: Stalin.

294 *Top:* Mussolini.
Bottom: Kemal Pasha.

295–96 Statistics compiled by the Carnegie Endowment for International Peace and published by the Oxford University Press under title, "The Direct and Indirect Cost of the World War."

297 Statistics from *The World Almanac,* 1933.

ACKNOWLEDGMENTS

Listed below are some of the sources from which photographs and documents for "The First World War" were obtained:

UNDERWOOD AND UNDERWOOD NEWS PHOTOS
INTERNATIONAL NEWS REEL
GLOBE PHOTOS
GILLIAMS PHOTOS
CARL EBERTH
PAUL THOMPSON
ACME NEWS PICTURES
U. S. SIGNAL CORPS
ROBERT SENNEKE
BRITISH IMPERIAL WAR MUSEUM
AMERICAN RED CROSS
W. GIRCKE
OSCAR TELLGMANN
KEYSTONE VIEW CO.
U. S. NAVY OFFICIAL PHOTOS
GEBR. HAEKEL
ITALIAN OFFICIAL PHOTOS
FRENCH OFFICIAL PHOTOS

MRS. COCKBURN-LANGE
NEW YORK TIMES
NEW YORK TRIBUNE (NOW HERALD TRIBUNE)
NEW YORK WORLD (NOW WORLD-TELEGRAM)
NEW YORK EVENING JOURNAL
NEW YORK SUN
NEW YORK AMERICAN
THE DAILY MAIL (LONDON)
LE FIGARO
BERLINER TAGEBLATT
NEUE FREIE PRESSE (VIENNA)